HISTORY OF INVENTION

AIR AND SPACE TRAVEL

HISTORY OF INVENTION

AIR AND SPACE TRAVEL

Chris Woodford

Facts On File, Inc.
132 West 31st Street
New York, NY 10001

Library of Congress Cataloging-in-Publication Data

Woodford, Chris
Air and space travel / Chris Woodford.
p. cm.
Summary: Outlines the development of air and space travel, from the winged flight of a monk in the year 1000 to modern fighter jets and helicopters.
Includes bibliographical references and index.
ISBN 0-8160-5436-3
1. Aeronautics—History—Juvenile literature. 2. Astronautics—History—Juvenile literature. [1. Aeronautics—History. 2. Astronautics—History.] I. Title.

TL547.W764 2003
629.1'09

2003058402

Facts On File books are available at special discounts when purchased in bulk quantities for businesses, associations, institutions, or sales promotions. Please call our Special Sales Department in New York at (212) 967-8800 or (800) 322-8755.

You can find Facts On File on the World Wide Web at http://www.factsonfile.com

For The Brown Reference Group plc:
Project Editor: Tom Jackson
Design: Bradbury and Williams
Picture Research: Becky Cox
Managing Editor: Bridget Giles
Consultant: L. Scott Miller, Professor of Aerospace Engineering, Wichita State University, Kansas.

Printed and bound in Singapore

10 9 8 7 6 5 4 3 2 1

The acknowledgments on page 96 form part of this copyright page. Every effort has been made to contact copyright holders of any material reproduced in this book. Any omission will be rectified in subsequent printings if notice is given to the publishers.

CONTENTS

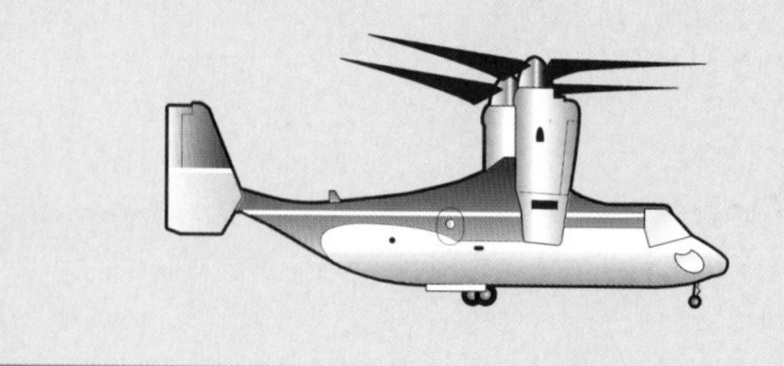

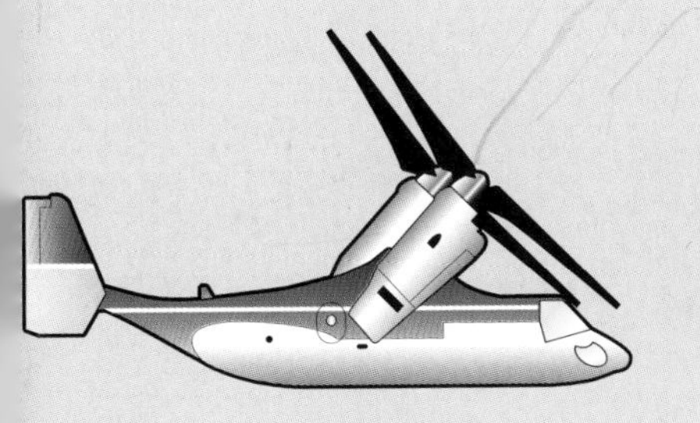

I WISH I COULD FLY

A 17th-century painting shows Icarus fall as his wings melt, while Daedalus, his father, stays aloft.

Flight has always held a special place in our imagination: People were dreaming about being able to fly thousands of years before airplanes were ever invented. Even in ancient civilizations, there were myths (traditional stories) about people who could fly. Many of these myths described flight not just as a special power but as something that could take chosen people to magical places.

Thousands of years ago, the ancient Mesopotamians (who lived where Iraq is today) told the legend of Etana, a shepherd who

The Flying Monk

People and society

Born in 980 C.E., Eilmer was a British monk who made a successful flight from Malmesbury Abbey in England when he was about 20 years old. With homemade wings attached to his arms and feet, he launched himself into the air from the top of the abbey's tower (above). Although he is reported to have flown a distance of around 600 feet (180 m), he broke both his legs on landing. Afterward Eilmer's abbot, the head of the abbey, forbade him from flying again. The monk walked with a limp for the rest of his life. A picture of the reckless young monk, complete with wings, can still be seen today in a stained glass window at the abbey.

flew to heaven on the back of an eagle. The story of Prince Ahmad, from the Persian (Iranian) tales the *Arabian Nights*, features a magic carpet that could fly.

Perhaps the most famous myth about flight is the ancient Greek legend of Daedalus and his son Icarus. While imprisoned in a labyrinth (maze), Daedalus made wings from wax and feathers, which he and Icarus used to fly to freedom. On their way home, however, Icarus flew too close to the Sun, the wax melted, and he fell into the sea and drowned.

FLIGHTS OF FANCY

Some people were not content to leave flight as the subject of legends, however, and wanted to fly themselves. Around 400 B.C.E., Greek mathematician Archytas is said to have built a model bird that flew using the power of steam. A hundred years later, the ancient Chinese perfected the art of flying kites although these aircraft did not carry people.

It is not clear who was the first person to attempt to fly. The honor may go to Spaniard Armen Firman, who made his attempt in 852 C.E. With a cloak cut into the shape of wings, he leapt from a tower in the city of Cordoba, flapping his arms. Fortunately, he survived the fall with few injuries. Twenty-five years later in the same city, inventor Abbas Ibn Firnas built a flying machine. Although his flight was successful, he injured his back trying to land. Firnas may have failed to fly far, but news of his attempt may have inspired many future flyers.

LIGHTER THAN AIR

Hot-air balloons are rarely used as a means of getting from A to B. They are generally flown for pleasure.

Today's aircraft take their inspiration from birds. Although they are heavier than air, birds generate a powerful force called lift, which counteracts the force of gravity. The first aircraft—balloons and airships—worked in a quite different way, however. They were lighter than air and floated above the ground.

No one knows who first had the idea to build hot-air balloons. About 2,000 years ago, Chinese children used to set fire to dry twigs that they had placed inside upturned eggshells. As the twigs burned, they heated the air inside the shells and made them fly into the air, much like miniature hot-air balloons. By 1200 C.E., the people of Mongolia were building hot-air balloons shaped like dragons and monsters that were flown during religious ceremonies.

THE SCIENCE OF FLOATING

The first hot-air balloons may have been built by trial and error, but they were, nevertheless, based on a firm scientific idea dating as far back as 200 B.C.E.

When Greek thinker Archimedes (287–212 B.C.E) leapt from his bath crying *Eureka!*—meaning "I've found it!"—he had discovered that objects float if they weigh less than the water they displace, or push out of the way. A British philosopher called Roger Bacon (1214–94 C.E.) thought that the same idea would also apply to the air. Bacon knew that ships floated on water because of Archimedes' principle. He thought that similar vessels might be built to float in midair.

However water and air seemed to be very different substances; why should they work in the same way? It was in the 17th century, with the pioneering work of Irish chemist Robert Boyle (1627–91), that people came to understand how this might be possible. Boyle showed that gases become less dense as they get hotter. (Density is a measure of how much matter is packed into a space.) This was the idea that eventually lifted humankind into the sky.

WE HAVE LIFT-OFF

It was not until 1783 that a hot-air balloon actually took off. French brothers Joseph-Michel (1740–1810) and Jacques-Étienne Montgolfier (1745–99) built a huge balloon out of linen and lined it with thin paper. With a straw and wood fire burning beneath, the balloon soared around 3,000 feet (900 m) into the air, prompting cries of amazement from the crowd of spectators. A few months later, the Montgolfiers constructed a bigger and better balloon and demonstrated it to the King and Queen of France, Louis XVI and

Nazca: The First Balloonists?

A few historians think the ancient Nazca people, who lived in Peru more than 1,500 years ago, could have been history's first balloonists. Between around 500 B.C.E. and 900 C.E., the Nazca created mysterious patterns in the desert. Some of the patterns are regular shapes, while others depicted animals and flowers. The patterns are all hundreds of feet long—so huge that they are fully visible only from high up.

There is a little evidence to suggest that the Nazca may have been the first people to fly. Their pottery shows pictures of balloons and kites, and their traditional textiles are so tightly woven that they could be used for balloons. In 1975, a group of U.S. balloonists made a balloon called *Condor I* (right). It rose almost 400 feet (120 m) in the air and stayed there for several minutes. This experiment shows the Peruvians just might have beaten the Montgolfiers into the air!

Marie Antoinette. This time, the balloon had three passengers—a duck, a rooster, and a sheep. All returned safely from the flight.

It was not just the animals who were lifted by the voyage. Buoyed with success, the Montgolfiers built a balloon to carry a human crew. On November 21, 1783, the Marquis d'Arlandes (1742–1809) and his friend François Pilâtre de Rozier (1757–85) became the first people to travel by balloon. Their voyage lasted 23 minutes and took them a distance of 5.5 miles (9 km) across Paris.

THE HYDROGEN BALLOON

People soon realized that heating up air was only one way of making a balloon float. Another method was to fill a balloon with a gas that was already lighter than air, and the great advantage of this was that the gas did not need to be heated. The most obvious gas to use was hydrogen, the lightest gas of all, and one that was readily produced by reacting metals with strong acids.

A month after the Montgolfier balloon's historic flight over Paris, two other Frenchmen, physicist Jacques-Alexandre Charles (1746–1823) and his friend Nicolas Robert, took to the skies in their hydrogen-filled balloon. Their voyage lasted two hours and took them nearly a mile (1.6 km) up into the sky!

BALLOONS BECOME AIRSHIPS

Although simple hot-air balloons are good at lifting things into the sky, once airborne, they go wherever the wind blows them. Modern balloonists use side vents and flaps to provide a little control, but balloons are still an impractical form of transportation.

Englishman Roger Bacon had speculated about ships traveling through the air, and a Frenchman, Henri Giffard (1825–82), made that possible in 1852. Instead of using a simple egg-shaped balloon, he built a cigar-shaped structure that could be relied on to move in only one direction. To this, he added a small steam engine that would turn a propeller and drive his balloon forward. The engine weighed about 350 pounds

The Montgolfier brothers and other onlookers witness the flight of the brothers' first hot-air balloon near Paris in 1783.

How things work

How Balloons Get Off the Ground

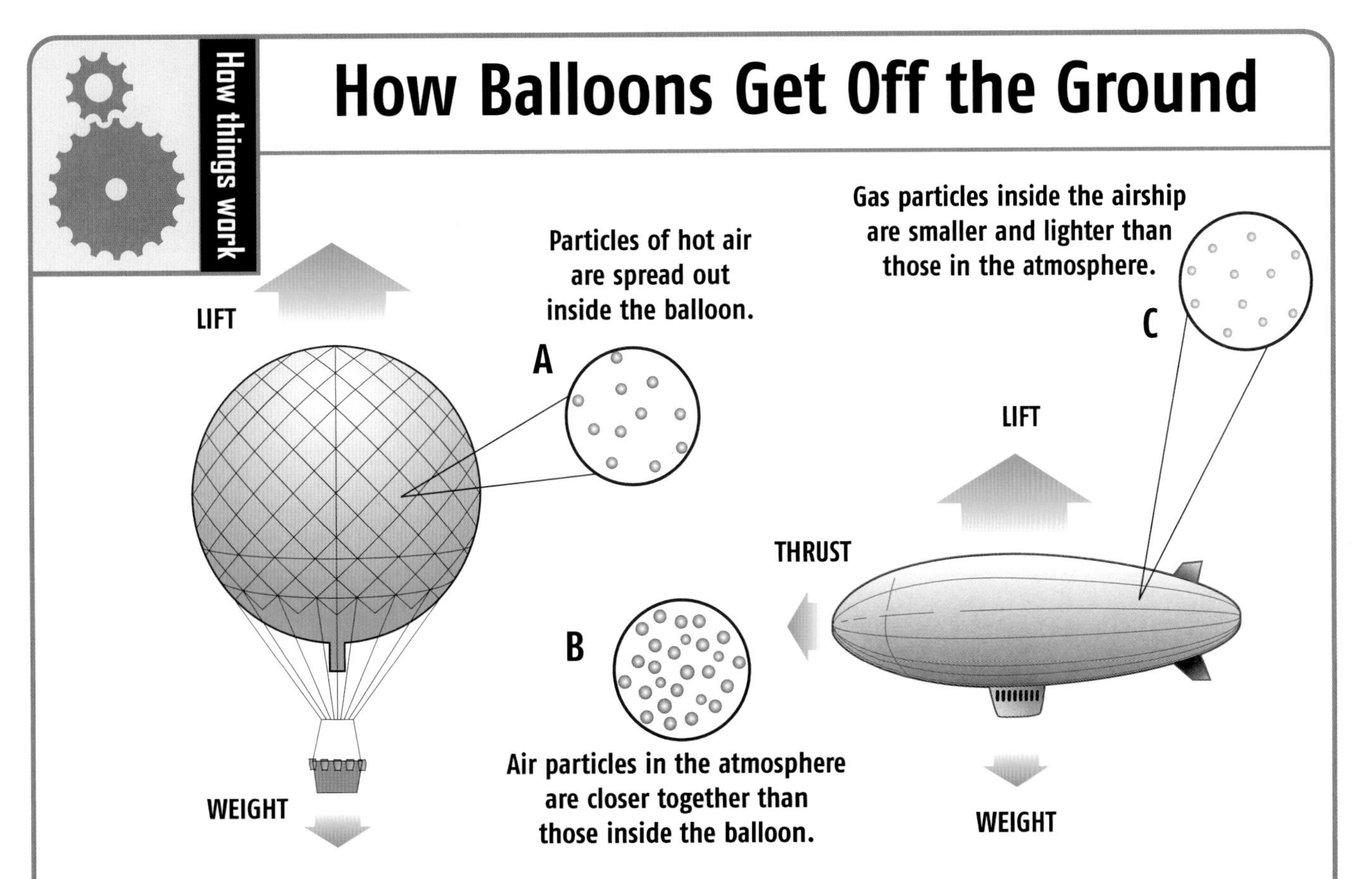

Archimedes found that something will float on the surface of water if it weighs less than the volume of water it displaces (pushes out of the way). The same idea applies to balloons and airships. Although an airship may be made of some materials that are denser than the air, the craft's entire volume (including all the gas it contains) weighs less than the same volume of air. If it weighs less than the air, it floats upward; if not, it stays firmly on the ground.

There are two ways of making the gas in a balloon weigh less than air. One way is to use hot air. Inside a hot-air balloon (**A**), the gas particles are spread out more than they are in the cooler air outside (**B**). The amount of hot air needed to inflate a balloon is less than the amount of cool air needed, and so the hot-air balloon is lighter. However, as the air cools down, more air is needed to keep the balloon inflated, and the heavier balloon sinks to the ground unless the air is heated up again (right).

The other way of achieving liftoff is to use a gas, such as hydrogen or helium, with particles that are lighter than those in air (**C**). In theory, balloons of this kind can stay in the air forever.

Zeppelin

The people gathered beneath this Zeppelin airship in Germany show how large these aircraft really were.

1. The vertical rudder steers this giant airship from side to side. Elevators are horizontal rudders that steered the airship up and down.

2. The pilot sat inside this tiny cabin slung under the airship.

3. Propeller engines produced the thrust force that moved the airship forward. They were also used to help steer.

(150 kg), or roughly as much as two human passengers. This extra weight meant that Giffard had to use a huge balloon that was 144 feet (44 m) long.

Giffard's airship was the most successful aircraft of its time. It reached a top speed of 6 mph (almost 10 km/h) and traveled 17 miles (27 km). His flying machine was the first dirigible, or maneuverable balloon. The word comes from the French word *diriger*, which means "to steer." Yet the aircraft was still at the mercy of any wind more powerful than its engine, so it could be used only in very calm weather. Fortunately, better forms of power soon became available. In 1872, German engineer Paul Haenlein used a lightweight internal-combustion engine (similar to the kind used in cars) fueled by hydrogen pumped from his balloon's gas bag. Eleven years later, two French brothers, Albert and Gaston Tissandier, powered a dirigible with an electric motor.

THE AGE OF THE ZEPPELIN

Airships did not become sophisticated enough to be practical forms of transportation until the beginning of the 20th

A meteorologist releases a hydrogen balloon from a weather station. Hydrogen balloons are used because they can fly higher than other types of balloons.

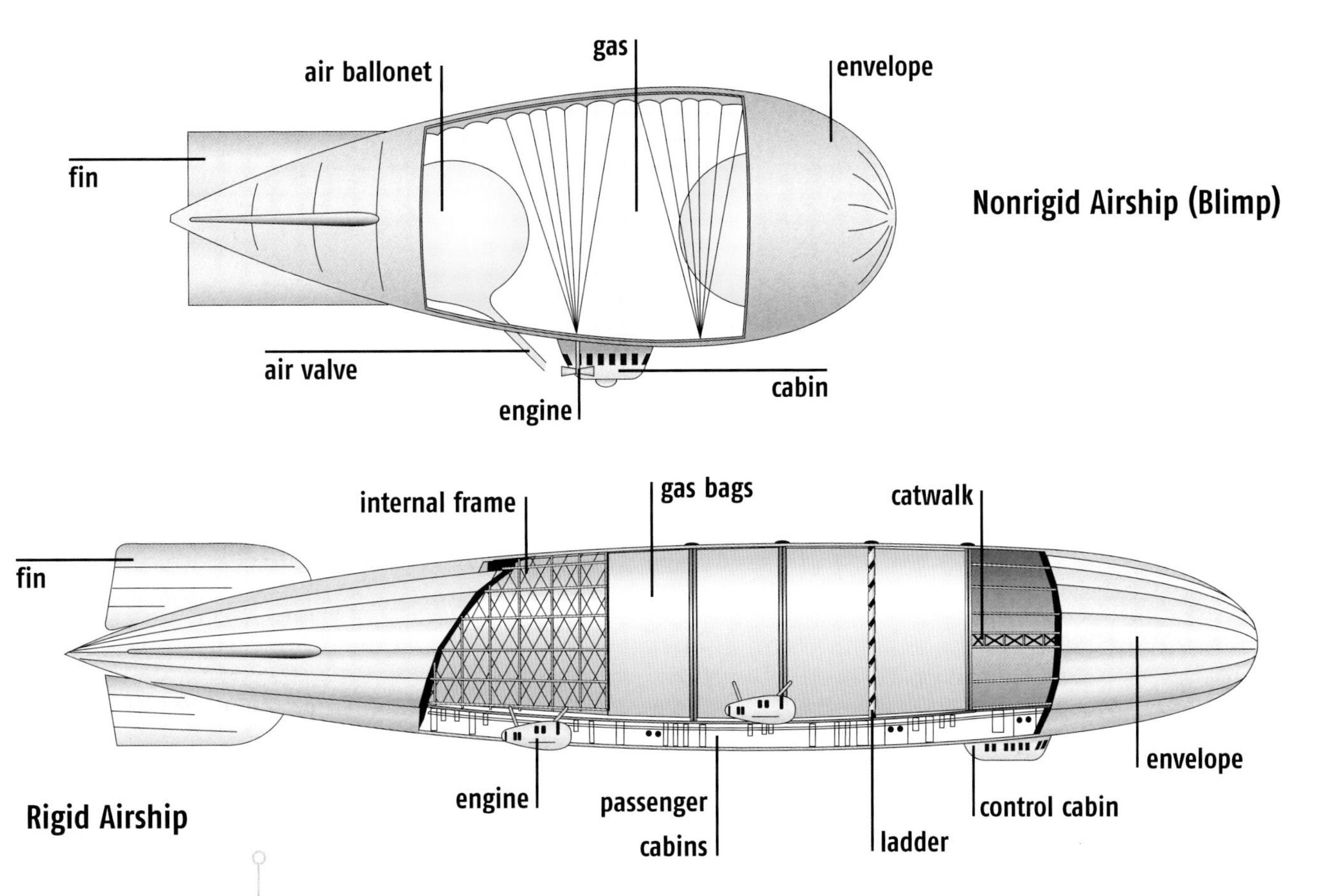

Nonrigid airships, or blimps, have no solid internal frame. Instead they take their shape when filled with gas. Air-filled ballonets control the blimp's altitude. Releasing air makes the ship rise, and pumping air back in causes the airship to sink. Rigid airships are much larger than blimps and have gas bags held inside a solid framework.

century. This was largely thanks to German army officer Count Ferdinand von Zeppelin (1838–1917). His biggest innovation was to add a lightweight but rigid frame to his dirigibles so they could be flown at much higher speeds and still remain possible to control. Zeppelins had two large propellers and, much like a ship, a keel and rudder that could steer them from side to side. Zeppelin's new "airships," as he called them, took some time to perfect. The first design contained 17 individual gas cells, made of rubber, that fitted inside a cylindrical framework covered in cloth. This early Zeppelin made its maiden voyage over Lake Konstanz in southern Germany on July 2, 1900, but plunged into the water after barely 17 minutes in the air. There were many more setbacks to come, but Zeppelin persevered and eventually made his first truly successful airship, the *LZ-4*, in 1908. The largest airship of its day, its gigantic rigid balloon was 446 feet (136 m) long (the length of about 25 cars parked bumper to bumper). It was so heavy that it needed 500,000 cubic feet (14,000 cubic meters) of hydrogen just to lift it off the ground. On July 4, 1908, it flew for 12 hours over Switzerland at a speed of 40 mph (60 km/h).

The first paying passengers could now travel long distances by air—years before winged airliners. By the time World War I broke out in 1914, around 34,000 people had traveled in Zeppelin's airships. By the end of the war, Zeppelins were managing to stay in the air for nearly 100 hours at a time. It was the war itself that prompted the development of bigger and better airships. The German military alone built 88 airships between 1914 and 1918. Because they could rise much higher than any airplane that had then been developed at that time, the military airships proved especially useful for dropping bombs. Their relatively quiet engines also gave them an element of surprise, as the people of London, England, found to their cost during a number of air raids.

RISE AND FALL OF THE AIRSHIP

By the end of the war, interest had returned to developing airships as a method of passenger travel. During the 1920s, when only a handful of airplanes were carrying passengers, airships had

People and society

The *Hindenberg* Disaster

The *Hindenberg* was the most spectacular airship ever built. Some 804 feet (245 m) long, it needed a massive balloon containing over 7,000,000 cubic feet (200,000 cubic meters) of hydrogen to lift it into the air. Once there, it could travel at speeds up to 78 mph (126 km/h). The *Hindenberg* made regular transatlantic crossings after its first voyage in 1936. Disaster struck on May 6, 1937, when it burst into flames as it landed at Lakehurst, New Jersey, (above) killing 36 of the 97 people aboard.

Floating Around the World

The *Breitling Orbiter 3* was the first air balloon to fly nonstop around the world. Crewed by Briton Brian Jones and Bertrand Piccard of Switzerland, the 200-foot- (60-m-) high balloon made its historic journey in 1999. Flying at about 42,000 feet (13,000 m)—slightly higher than a modern jet airliner—*Breitling Orbiter* took 19 days to circle the Earth. Taking off from Switzerland, the balloon rode the jet stream, strong 120-mph (200-km/h) winds found high in the atmosphere. *Breitling Orbiter* followed the equator, traveling 28,431 miles (45,755 km) before finally touching down again in the Egyptian desert.

Breitling Orbiter (right) was filled with both hot air and helium. A helium cell was surrounded by a jacket of hot air. By controlling the temperature of this outer jacket, the balloon's crew could control their altitude and catch the most favorable winds.

helium balloon
valve
helium cell
hot-air jacket
crew cabin

already become the first airliners. Then disaster struck. Three military airships built by the U.S. Navy crashed and exploded between 1925 and 1935. In 1930, the luxurious British airship *R101* crashed on its maiden voyage in France, killing all but 6 of its 54 passengers. The final blow came in 1937, when Germany's mighty transatlantic airship *Hindenburg* crashed in flames in New Jersey. After this disaster, people finally realized that airships packed full of highly flammable hydrogen gas were little more than explosions waiting to happen.

Dirgibles and balloons filled with nonflammable gases such as helium are still used today. Helium, the second lightest gas, is very safe to handle. Since it is completely unreactive, helium cannot burn. However, because of its inertness, helium was not identified until the late 19th century and not purified on a large scale for many more years.

Despite this safe alternative to hydrogen, the spectacular crashes of the 1920s and 1930s ended the dreams of inventors like Zeppelin. They had imagined fleets of giant airships carrying people around the world. Fortunately, the development of winged aircraft would soon make those dreams redundant, with giant airplanes carrying hundreds of passengers thousands of miles.

HEAVIER THAN AIR

Otto Lilienthal prepares to fly from a hill near Rhinow, Germany, in one of his many gliders. The glider's wings were pulled into the correct curved shape by the many wires.

Balloons and airships flew by being lighter than air, but that is not the only way of lifting an aircraft off the ground. Some early pioneers believed they could fly by making machines with large flapping wings. Even the great Italian inventor Leonardo da Vinci (1452–1519) sketched impractical flying machines of this kind. However, another Italian scientist, Giovanni A. Borelli (1608–1679), eventually proved that people would need enormous wings to lift their bodies off the ground, and that our chest muscles would not be powerful enough to flap them. Fortunately, there is another way of getting things airborne, even when they are heavier than air.

PIONEERS OF AERODYNAMICS

The properties of gases explain how a heavy balloon or airship can stay airborne. In much the same way, the physics of moving air, or aerodynamics, explains how the wings of a moving airplane can lift it off the ground. The pioneer of aerodynamics was a Swiss scientist named Daniel Bernoulli (1700–1782). Bernoulli found that the pressure of a moving liquid or gas goes down

as its speed increases. British aristocrat Sir George Cayley (1773 –1857) used Bernoulli's idea to develop flying machines that were heavier than air.

Cayley had been interested in flying since he was a boy. He concentrated on using Bernoulli's principle to produce an airplane that used fixed wings to give it lift—his wings had a curved shape called an airfoil. By the age of 26, Cayley had worked out the basic design of his flying machine, and every airplane built since has been based on this design. Cayley's machine had a fuselage (central body), fixed wings either side, and a tail with elevators, flaps to make the plane climb or dive in the sky, and a rudder for steering from side to side.

Lightweight engines had not been invented at this time, so Cayley's flying machines were unpowered gliders. The first one flew in 1804, though it was only a model. Cayley spent the next 50 years improving his design, and also published the first book on aerodynamics. Eventually, in 1853, he tested out his ideas by launching a large glider, piloted by a servant, off a steep hill. This was the first piloted flight.

Soon others were developing their own unpowered aircraft. Frenchman Jean-Marie Le Bris built his "artificial albatross" glider in 1857. Birds inspired other glider makers, too. German engineer Otto Lilienthal (1848–1896) had started off with flapping-wing machines before

A model of Sir George Cayley's "aerial carriage," an early aircraft design based on spinning wings and propellers. Cayley's later designs looked a lot more like modern airplanes.

concentrating his efforts on the design of fixed-wing gliders. After making around 2,000 successful flights, he was killed when one of his gliders crashed. Fortunately, he recorded his ideas in a book called *The Flight of Birds as the Basis of Flying*.

THE WRIGHT BROTHERS

Lilienthal's work inspired other pioneers of flight, none more so than Wilbur Wright (1867–1912) and Orville Wright (1871–1948) from Dayton, Ohio. The Wright brothers were bicycle makers and printers, but their real passion was aviation. As boys, they had loved to fly kites, and as young men, they built many large and sophisticated gliders. In 1903, they made a huge advance: By adding a very lightweight gasoline engine to a large glider, they built the first self-propelled airplane. The age of aviation had begun.

Key inventions

Kites: The First Aircraft?

Gliders and airplanes were not the first heavier-than-air craft; that distinction probably belongs to the humble kite (above). Ancient Chinese people were making kites around 300 or 400 B.C.E., but the art of kite flying became part of modern aviation history through the work of Australian draftsman Lawrence Hargrave (1850–1915). Many of his ideas were incorporated into the designs of early airplanes. Biplanes (two-winged aircraft), for example, bear a strong resemblance to the box kites that Hargrave designed. Hargrave himself became one of the first air passengers in 1894 when he was accidentally lifted 16 feet (5 m) into the air by four of his box kites!

How things work

The Forces on a Plane

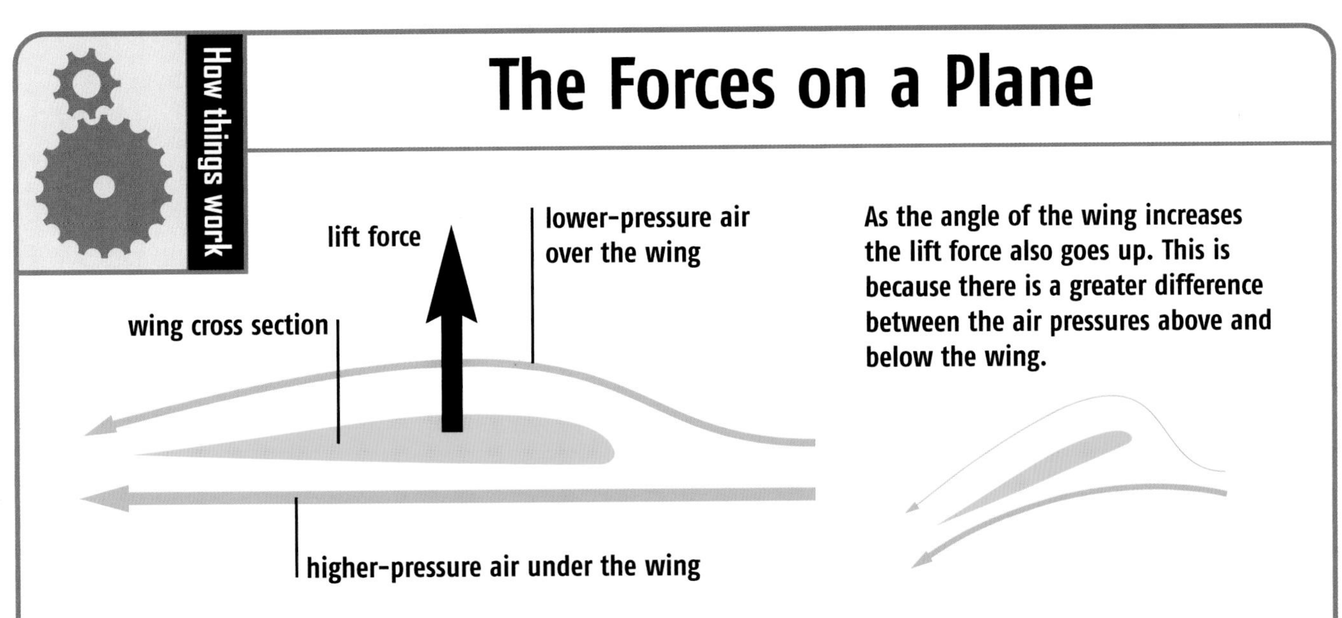

As the angle of the wing increases the lift force also goes up. This is because there is a greater difference between the air pressures above and below the wing.

The Airfoil Effect

When air rushes over the curved upper surface of an airplane's wing, it travels faster and farther than the air passing underneath. According to Bernoulli's principle, this means the air above the wing is at a lower pressure than the air beneath. The difference in pressure provides an upward force called lift. If the air travels fast enough, the lift force exceeds the weight of the wing and the rest of the plane. When this happens the plane takes off into the air. Known as the airfoil effect, this crucial piece of aerodynamics is used by all aircraft from box kites to jet fighters.

The Four Forces

Flying a plane is a two-way tug-of-war between four different forces acting at right angles to one another. Gravity constantly pulls a plane toward the ground, giving the aircraft its weight. This force is opposed by lift, the upward force generated by the plane's curved wings. During takeoff, lift exceeds the force of gravity so the plane rises; during landing, the opposite occurs. If gravity and lift were the only forces acting on a plane, it would move straight up and down or hover in midair. However, air must rush over and under the wings to create the lift force, so a plane has engines to push it forward through the air. The force produced by the engines is called thrust. The faster a plane flies, however, the more it is pulled backward by air resistance—a force often known as drag.

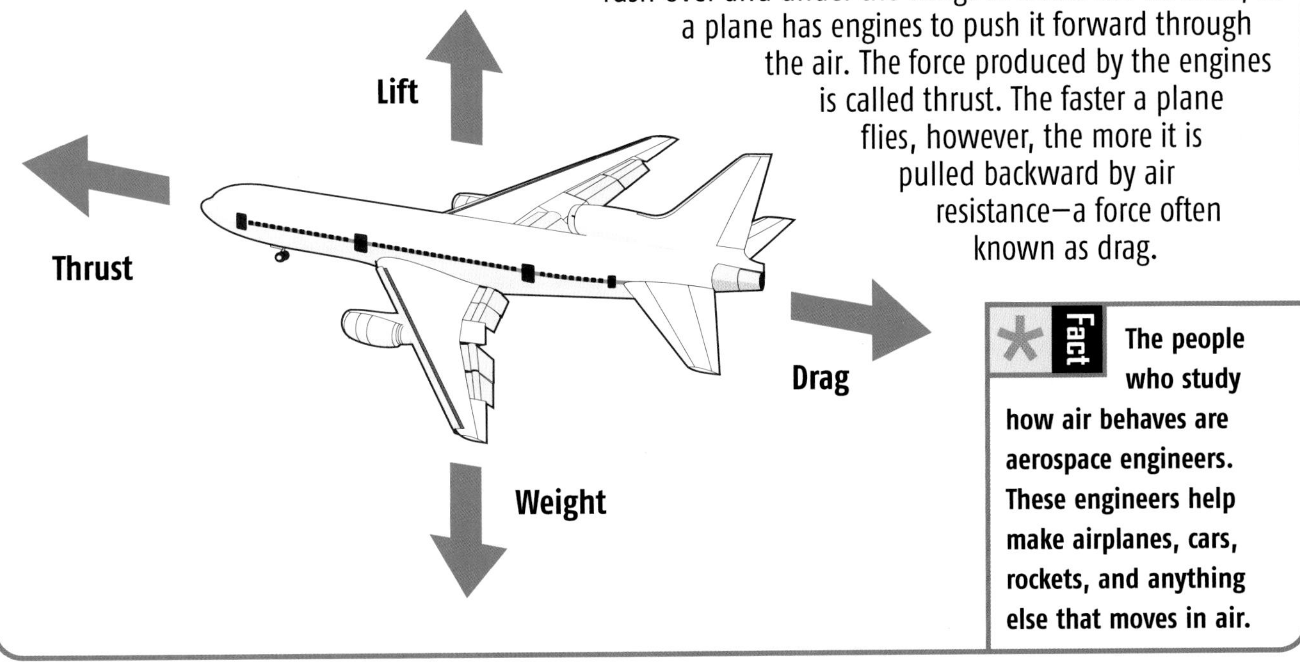

Fact

The people who study how air behaves are aerospace engineers. These engineers help make airplanes, cars, rockets, and anything else that moves in air.

THE FIRST FLIGHT

Wilbur Wright (right) looks on as his brother Orville pilots **Flyer** *into the air for the first time. The simple track used as a runway runs over the sandy beach from the left of the picture.*

December 17, 1903, was a cold and windy day at Kitty Hawk beach in North Carolina, but no one would remember it for the weather. Conditions turned out to be just right for the greatest day in aviation history, the moment when brothers Wilbur and Orville Wright flew into the history books in the world's first airplane.

By today's standards, *Flyer* could hardly have been less sophisticated. Its two wings, roughly 40 feet (12 m) from end to end, were made of flimsy wood and covered in tight canvas. The plane stood on runners rather than wheels, and there was no seat either—the pilot had to lie face down on the lower wing.

Flyer's greatest innovation was probably its lightweight gasoline engine, which drove two propellers mounted at the rear of the plane. Gasoline engines, like the ones used in cars, had been invented less than twenty years before, and the Wrights had written to

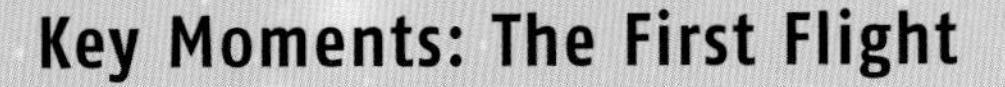

several engine companies asking their help in building an engine light but powerful enough for an airplane. No one wanted to help them, so the brothers decided to design and build their own.

The engine was a triumph. Powered by gasoline and weighing only 180 pounds (81 kg), it produced more than enough power to lift the 750-pound (338-kg) aircraft, which included the weight of the pilot, into the air.

Since it was the first airplane, there were no runways for the Wrights to launch their homespun craft. The flat beach at Kill Devil Hill near Kitty Hawk was perfect for the job, however, and the brothers had made several glider flights there the year before. They mounted their plane on a simple cart that rolled along a wooden railroad. At 10:35 A.M., Orville climbed aboard and lay down in the pilot's position. The propellers had been turning for several minutes when Wilbur finally released the rope that was holding the plane still. The plane growled forward into the wind, slowly enough for Wilbur to run alongside and steady its wings. About 40 feet (12 m) down the track, *Flyer* took off, climbing to 10 feet (3 m) off the ground. The historic flight took Orville Wright a grand distance of about 120 feet (37 m) and lasted only 12 seconds. Later that day, Wilbur took the controls, and he flew for just under a minute. Within two years, however, the brothers had built a plane that could fly nearly 25 miles (40 km).

Flyer

1. Fuel tank attached by tube to engine.

2. Water-filled radiator keeps engine cool.

3. Chains attach engine to propellers.

4. Wires joining wings are attached to a harness around the pilot's hips. The pilot pulls the wires to warp the shape of wings and steer the plane.

5. Propellers fitted at the rear of the plane.

REACHING FOR THE SKY

The German designer of this 1909 flying machine thought that the three large wings would allow his aircraft to fly higher than others. His creation, however, never got off the ground, crashing during its first takeoff.

The Wright brothers' flight was an extraordinary achievement, although planes that could fly for only a few seconds were not going to get people very far. Bigger and better aircraft were soon in development, thanks to the pressing needs of wartime, the competition between the new airplane manufacturers, and the technological advances that were rapidly being made each year.

THE AGE OF THE BIPLANE

Flyer was an example of a biplane since it had two parallel wings, one on top of the other. There was much to recommend this design. With struts and bracing wires holding the two wings together, a biplane managed to be both light enough to fly yet strong enough to withstand the stresses of flight once it was airborne. Two wings together also gave twice as much lift as one wing, so biplanes were far easier to get off the ground.

Making wings strong enough to fly was one of the major challenges that occupied early airplane designers. Some used even more rigid wing structures based on box kites. Others got their inspiration elsewhere. U.S. glider pioneer Octave Chanute (1832–1910) had originally been a construction engineer. He began to use crisscrossed trusses, like those that strengthened the buildings and bridges he had worked on, to make his biplane gliders more rigid.

An airplane with flimsy wings is hard to control because even the slightest change in wing shape makes it change direction. With their rigid wings, Chanute's gliders were easy to control. They were so safe that Chanute himself made more than 2,000 flights without a single accident—quite a feat for a pioneer aviator.

DAREDEVILS OF THE SKIES

Early biplanes developed through two kinds of battles. One was the fight for control of the skies above the battlefields of World War I (1914–18); the other was a more good-natured battle between the many airplane designers who were following in the Wright brothers' flightpath.

Record-breaking flyers won huge cash prizes. In 1910, American air ace Glenn H. Curtiss (1878–1930) won the then enormous amount of $10,000 for flying from Albany to New York City. Other aviation pioneers risked their lives making even greater journeys. In 1911, another American, Calbraith Perry

Louis Blériot shows off one of his early monoplanes in the 1900s. The French aviator built many aircraft but most were destroyed in crashes. In 1912, he became the first person to fly across the English Channel. He was also the first person to take to the skies with two passengers.

Rodgers (1879–1912), became the first person to cross the United States when he traveled from Long Island, New York, to Long Beach, California, in 49 days. (Only about 85 hours of this was spent in the air, however.) The greatest challenge of the age was flying across the ocean between Europe and America. In 1911, two British aviators, John Alcock (1892–1919) and Arthur Brown (1886–1948), were the first to overcome this hurdle, when they flew for 16.5 hours from Newfoundland to Ireland.

People's interest in flying was stimulated by spectacular public demonstrations. Both Glenn Curtiss and Wilbur Wright made several public flights. These exhibitions soon evolved into regular meets, which intensified competition between airplane pioneers yet further. The first international event was held in Reims, France, in 1909, while the first U.S. meet took place in Los Angeles early the following year.

ONE WING OR TWO?

The strength and controllability of biplanes came at a price. Their two pairs of wings, plus their numerous interconnecting struts and braces, caused a great deal of air resistance. This slowed planes down and increased their fuel consumption, limiting both how fast and how far they could fly. These problems were particularly noticeable in warplanes: Bombers needed to fly as far as possible, while fighters needed to be fast and highly maneuverable to avoid being shot down.

The first monoplanes—planes with a single wing—had been designed at the same time as biplanes. Although monoplanes could fly faster, their single flimsy wing made them harder to get off

Charles Lindbergh (marked with an X*) stands beside his record-breaking monoplane* Spirit of St. Louis. *In 1927, the U.S. aviator won $25,000 when he became the first person to fly solo across the Atlantic Ocean. The flight from New York to Paris took 34 hours and made Lindbergh a hero in the United States and around the world.*

How things work

The Basics of Aviation

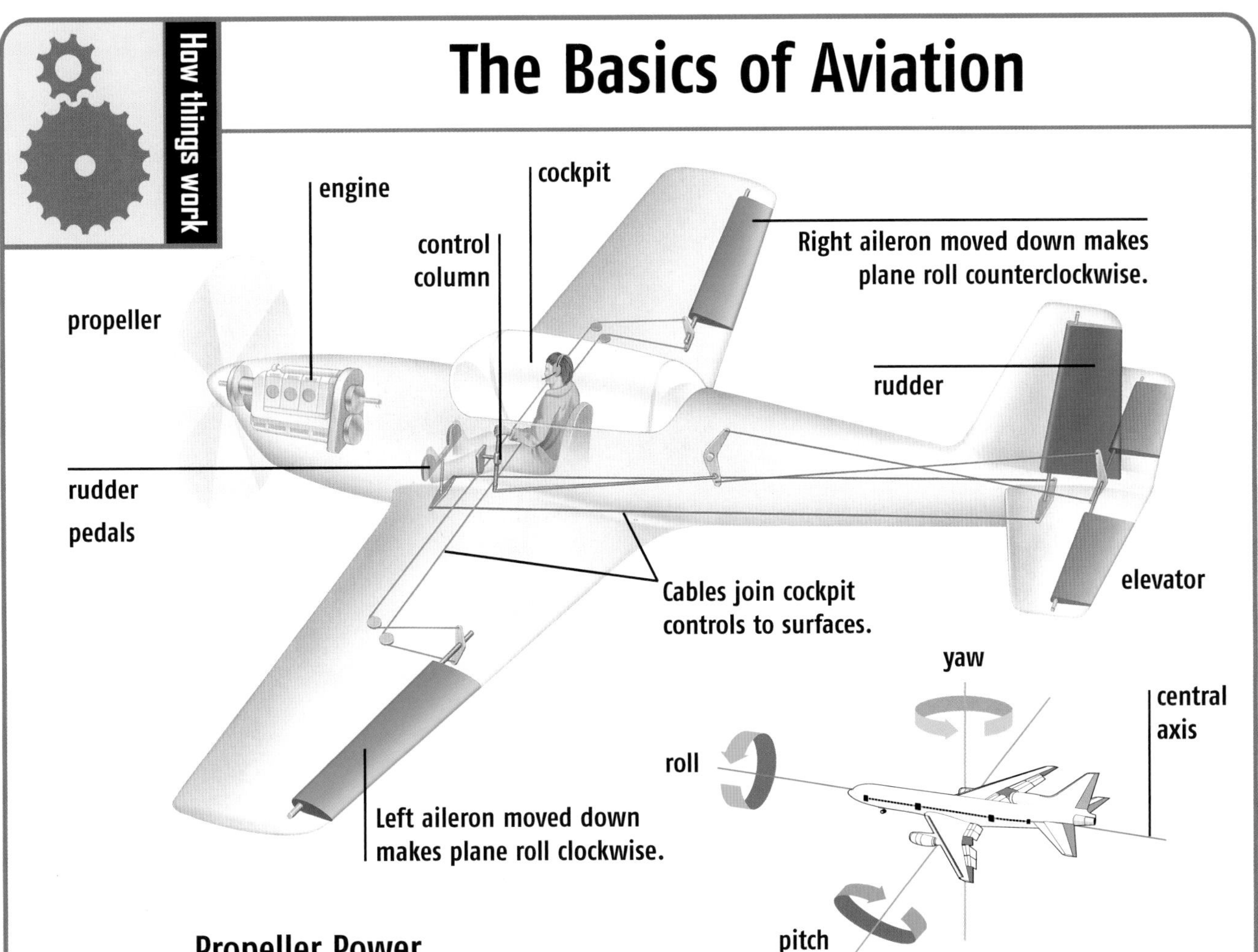

Propeller Power

A force that pushes backward can shoot something forward. This explains why guns recoil backward when they shoot bullets forward, and why skateboarders shoot forward when they kick backward off a sidewalk.

It also explains how propellers push aircraft through the sky. The propeller pushes air backward in a massive draft that propels the plane forward. Each propeller is turned around by its own gasoline engine that works in the same way as the one used in an automobile. Instead of turning the wheels, the engine spins the propeller at very high speeds. Unlike car engines, many propeller plane engines are "radial," with all the pistons arranged in a circle around a central drive shaft.

The propeller is no less important than the engine that drives it. Its blades have a curved airfoil shape that create the thrust force. In some cases blades can be tilted at different angles to control thrust and the aircraft's speed.

Steering System

Once in the air, modern airplanes steer using movable flaps on the wing and tail, called control surfaces. When these surfaces are moved into the air current, the air pushes against them, and the aircraft changes direction. The rudder is moved by pedals in the cockpit and turns the plane from side to side. The motion the rudder produces is called yaw. The plane's up and down motion, or pitch, is controlled by elevators on the tail. The elevators are raised when the pilot pulls on the control column, making the plane climb. Pushing the controls produces a dive. The ailerons are the flaps on the back of the wing. They always move in the opposite direction to each other, when the control column is moved from side to side. When one is raised, the other is lowered. The ailerons make the aircraft roll, or move around a central axis. Pilots must use all the controls at once to steer.

the ground. They were also very hard to steer in the air. A design innovation known as spar-and-rib construction made it possible to build very rigid monoplane wings. The spars, which were struts running along the length of the wing, carried most of the weight while the curved ribs gave the wings their crucial airfoil shape.

The possibilities of monoplane design were demonstrated not long after the Wright brothers took to the sky in their biplane. French engineer Louis Blériot (1872–1936) built a successful monoplane in 1907 and flew it across the English Channel between England and France.

Yet biplanes dominated the skies until the 1930s. The balance finally began to shift in 1927, when Charles Lindbergh made his famous solo flight across the Atlantic from New York to Paris in his monoplane, *Spirit of St. Louis*.

WARPLANES

Air combat was more important in World War II (1939–45) than it had been in World War I, when the possibilities of bombing an enemy from the sky had barely been investigated. Nothing speeds the progress of technology faster than war, and as war loomed in the 1930s, the world's air forces rapidly updated their warplanes. Their wooden biplanes that were similar to those built by the Wright brothers were replaced with all-metal monoplanes that were stronger, sleeker, and faster.

But the need to fly faster and farther with ever greater loads stretched airplane design—and their engines, in particular—to the limit. One thing soon became apparent: If airplanes were to develop any further, they would need a new and much more powerful type of engine. That next innovation proved to be just around the corner.

People and society

Amelia Earhart

Not all the great air pioneers were men. One year after Charles Lindbergh's pioneering transatlantic voyage, American aviator Amelia Earhart (1898–1937) became the first woman to make the same voyage, albeit as a passenger. In 1932, Earhart (above) flew the same crossing alone in just 13.5 hours and, three years later, was the first woman to cross the Pacific. In 1937, Earhart attempted to circle the globe. After many flights between California and New Guinea, Earhart and her navigator, Frederick Noonan, disappeared on the longest leg of their journey. It is most likely they ran out of fuel while trying to find their destination–remote Howland Island in the Pacific–and crashed into the ocean.

Key inventions

Parachutes

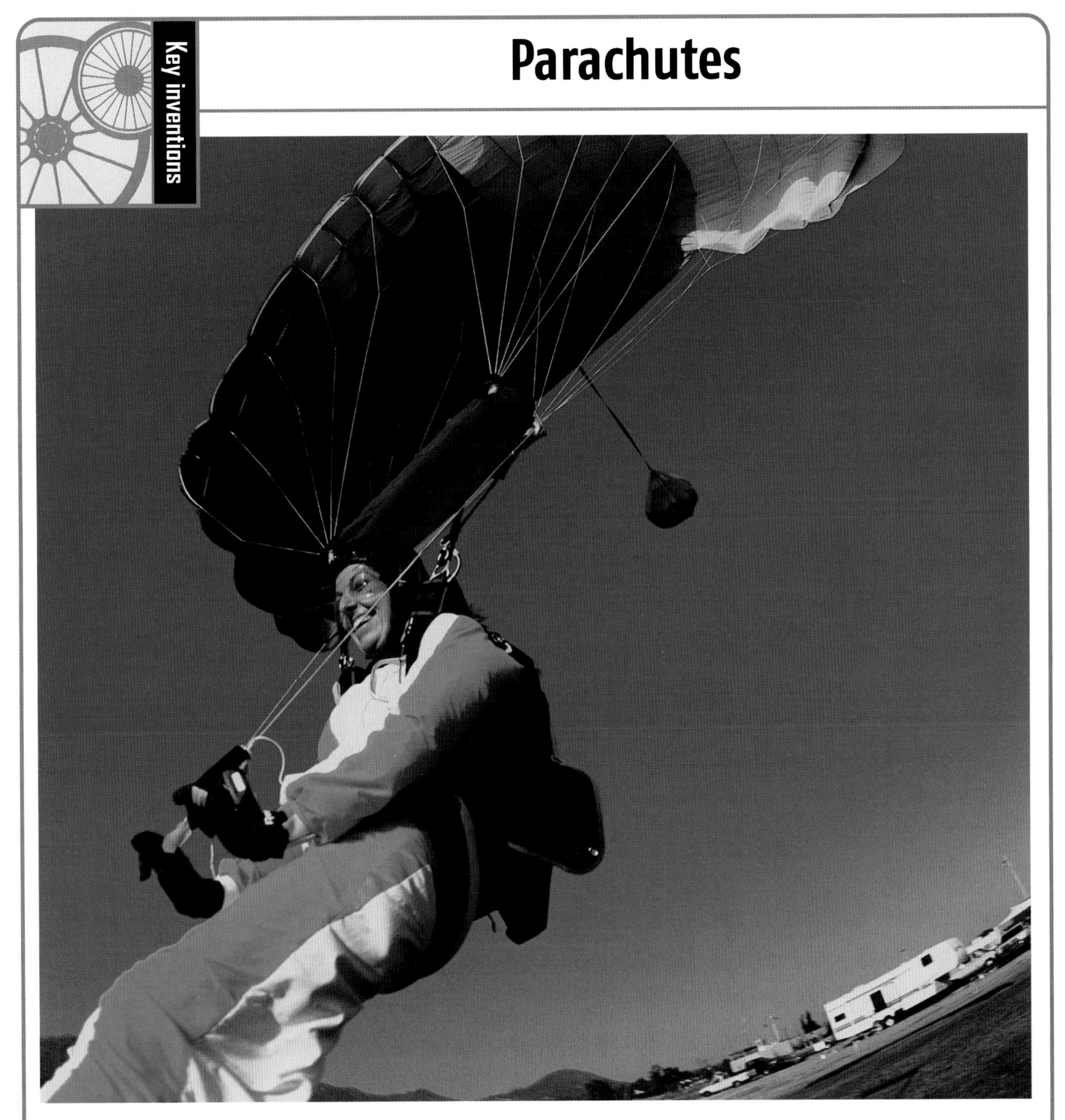

Pushing back the limits of air travel is a risky business, and many pioneering aviators have been killed when they lost control of their aircraft or it was damaged in some way. The only way back to the safety of solid ground is to jump out of the plane and float back to earth using a parachute. Parachutes work by trapping a pocket of air under a large fabric canopy (above). The user hangs by straps from the canopy as it falls to the ground. Air rushing past must force its way around the canopy, and creates a large, upward drag force. The drag opposes the force of gravity that is pulling the user downward, and, as a result, the fall is slowed to a safer speed.

Parachutes were first tested by Chinese inventors in the 12th century. Their chutes were more like large, rigid umbrellas than modern ones, but they could break a person's fall. The first fabric parachute was used by French physicist Sébastian Lenormand, who parachuted from a tower in 1783.

WORLD WAR AIRCRAFT

This German warplane from World War I has three sets of wings and is consequently known as a triplane. Like a biplane, triplanes are very stable in flight, but they can climb even more quickly because of the extra lift produced by the third wing.

It is an unfortunate fact that the history of aviation owes much of its development to war. Wilbur and Orville Wright built the world's first military airplane for the U.S. Army in 1909. One year later, all of the world's great armies had airplanes, although they used them only for spying. The warplane was invented almost by accident three years before the outbreak of World War I. On October 30, 1911, an Italian pilot observing enemy forces in Libya dropped four hand grenades over the side of his plane and promptly invented the bomber.

During World War I, aircraft became heavily armed fighting machines. Dutch-U.S. aircraft designer Anthony Fokker (1890–1939) took this idea a step further by connecting the engine and the machine gun together so the bullets were timed to travel between the spinning blades. Fokker was one of the most successful builders of fighter planes—such as the Fokker triplane—during World War I, and he pioneered the use of frames of welded-steel tubes to make light but strong fuselages.

Other famous fighter planes during this period included Britain's Sopwith Camel, while pioneering bombers included the German Junkers, which was the first all-metal monoplane. The United States military made few planes of

The Spitfire

1. The Spitfire flew at over 350 mph (563 km/h) at heights of 40,000 feet (12,000 m), and the pilot sat inside a cockpit protected by a canopy.

2. Machine guns on the wings were the Spitfire's main weapons.

3. Like other World War II fighters, the Spitfire was powered by a single powerful piston engine.

4. The fuselage was covered in a thin skin of metal, not fabric.

A B-17 bomber raids a German airfield in 1945. This aircraft was named the Flying Fortress because it was heavily armored and had several machine guns.

this type, although it did build thousands of Curtiss Jennie training aircraft.

During the 1930s, several nations realized that aircraft would be crucial in any future conflict, and began building more powerful bombers to attack ground targets. They also developed fighters, planes designed to destroy enemy aircraft in flight.

Aircraft did indeed play a crucial role in World War II. The first great air battle, the Battle of Britain, took place in the summer of 1940. As the German army prepared to invade Britain, the *Luftwaffe* (German air force) began bombing England. However, the invasion plans were dashed by Britain's Royal Air Force (RAF). RAF pilots, including aviators from across the world, flew Hawker Hurricanes and Supermarine Spitfires in dogfights with German Focke-Wulf 190 and Messerschmitt 109 fighters.

Another major air event of the war was the Japanese bombing of the U.S. military base at Pearl Harbor, Hawaii. This prompted the U.S. government to manufacture a huge number of modern warplanes. Famous fighters included the Lockheed Lightning, North American Mustang, and Grumman Hellcat, while bombers such as the Boeing B-17 Flying Fortress also came into service. The war's deadliest planes were undoubtedly the Boeing B-29 Superfortresses, which dropped atomic bombs on Japan in 1945.

THE AGE OF SPEED

An F-14 Tomcat climbs with its afterburners blasting flames from the jet engines. The afterburners give the fighter an extra boost when needed.

During the first few decades of their existence, airplanes flew ever faster and farther. In 1903, the Wright brothers' *Flyer* had a top speed of about 30 mph (50 km/h). When World War I began 11 years later, planes were flying roughly twice this speed; by the end of that war in 1918, their speed had doubled again to around 130 mph (209 km/h). Such great advances were made between the two world wars that by the time World War II broke out in 1939, fighter planes were reaching speeds up to 350 mph (563 km/h). Each new increase in speed put more and more stress on an airplane's engine, wings, and fuselage. One question preoccupied every airplane designer at this time: Just how fast could an aircraft fly without tearing itself apart completely?

THE LIMITS OF AIR SPEED

The pioneers of airplane design learned a great deal about the way objects move through air. They also began to learn how air behaves when machines cut through it at high speed.

They soon discovered that there was a limit to how fast an aircraft powered by a propeller could fly. At relatively low speeds, air flows

Space shuttle:
115 miles (184 km)

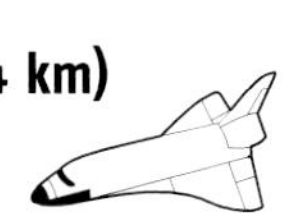

Spyplane:
More than 80,000 ft (24,500 m)

Concorde:
70,000 ft (21,000 m)

Fighter-bomber:
50,000 ft (15,000 m)

Airliner:
40,000 ft (12,000 m)

Private jet:
24,000 ft (7,500 m)

Light aircraft:
10,000 ft
(3,000 m)

Mount Everest: 29,002 ft (8,840 m)

Airplanes are designed to fly at different heights. High-speed aircraft cruise at high altitudes, where the air is thinner.

smoothly around an airplane's fuselage, and as it rushes over the wings, it gives the lift that keeps a plane in the air. All this begins to change at higher speeds. Air particles get squeezed together increasing resistance (drag force). As the plane flies faster, the smooth flow of air around the plane becomes increasingly turbulent. The plane gets buffeted more and more, loses lift, and eventually flies out of control. Air resistance becomes a problem first at the propellers, which are naturally the fastest-moving parts of any aircraft. Air turbulence sets a limit to how fast a propeller can turn and continue to push the airplane through the air.

ROCKETING FORWARD

During the 1920s and 1930s, airplane designers had realized that if they were to make their dream machines fly any faster, they would need a completely different type of engine. One promising possibility seemed to be the rocket engine, and this was developed by engineers in both the United States and Germany.

In 1928, German engineer Alexander M. Lippisch (1894–1976) added two rocket engines to a glider and so created the world's first rocket plane. This design eventually became a rocket-powered fighter plane: the Messerschmitt Me-163 Komet. Under the leadership of Wernher von Braun (1912–77), the Germans went on to develop the first rocket-propelled missiles, which they used in World War II. The German engineers benefited greatly from rocket research carried out in the 1920s and '30s by American inventor Robert Hutchings Goddard (1882 –1945), whose work was treated with less importance in his own country.

In theory at least, rocket engines could propel airplanes to previously undreamed of speeds; in practice, they created a whole new set of problems for the aircraft designer. Rocket planes are expensive to run and are also very difficult to launch. And, no less importantly, few pilots were willing to sit aboard what was, in reality, something like a huge firework. Rocket engines were simply not practical for powering airplanes.

THE COMING OF THE JET

Fortunately, another type of engine met the need. In 1910, only seven years after the Wright brothers made their pioneering

Key inventions

Rocket Plane

One of the most unusual planes developed in the prelude to World War II was the Messerschmitt Me-163 Komet (above)—the world's first ever fully operational rocket plane. Its two major advantages were a very fast rate of climbing and a top speed of over 600 mph (970 km/h)—as fast as a modern jet airliner and twice as fast as enemy fighters. It had a number of drawbacks, however. Apart from being very hard to fly, it used massive amounts of fuel (just like modern space rockets), so it could not fly far. It also had a tendency to explode without warning. The Komet went into production in July 1944 and fewer than 300 had been built when the war ended the following year.

Although they were flying the fastest aircraft of the age, Komet pilots were not very successful in combat. One squadron destroyed only nine enemy planes but lost 14 of their own planes.

One of the first jet airplanes to be produced, the British Gloster Meteor, saw action in the last few months of World War II. It first went into combat to shoot down German V-1s—unpiloted flying bombs powered by jets.

flight, French-Romanian scientist Henri-Marie Coanda (1885–1972) designed the first airplane to be powered by a jet of air. However, this aircraft caught fire on takeoff. It was another twenty years before a practical jet engine was invented and another decade after that before a jet aircraft flew.

Two figures stand out in the early development of jet aircraft. British engineer Frank Whittle (1907–96) invented the jet engine in 1928. The first person to build a jet-powered aircraft, however, was German engineer Hans Pabst von Ohain (1911–98). The Heinkel He-178 he designed finally took to the sky on August 27, 1939.

Jet fighters were developed too late to play much of a role in World War II, however, although jet-powered aircraft such as Britain's Gloster Meteor (powered by a Whittle engine) did take on Germany's Messerschmitt Me-262s (powered by the rival engine developed by Ohain) toward the end of the conflict. Britain and Germany were the only nations to have jet-powered planes during the war, but other nations, including the United States and the Soviet Union, developed jet aircraft soon afterward.

GOING SUPERSONIC

Jet engines broke the speed limits of propeller-driven aircraft and carried planes through the skies far faster than ever before. The Messerschmitt Me-262 could reach previously unthinkable speeds up to 550 mph (885 km/h). As aircraft flew ever faster, pilots found themselves approaching a speed limit no one thought they would be able to exceed—the speed of sound (roughly 660 mph or 1,062 km/h). Some people thought traveling faster than sound would destroy an airplane and kill its pilot because an airplane at this speed generates a huge amount of turbulence; others were not so sure. There was only one way to find out.

Engineers at the U.S Bell Aircraft Company in the United States set themselves this new challenge in the late 1940s. They knew bullets traveled faster than sound so they designed their plane, the *X-1*, to have roughly the same shape as a 0.50-caliber bullet. Instead of using one of the

People and society

Ahead of Their Time

While their countries battled in World War II, Britain's Frank Whittle (right) and Germany's Hans Pabst von Ohain fought a battle of quite a different kind to develop jet propulsion.

Whittle was a bright student who had sketched out his ideas for a jet engine in 1928, as part of a college thesis, at the age of just 21. No one took the young Whittle seriously, and he failed to win support either from the British government or from industry.

Whittle then formed his own company, Power Jets Limited, to develop the ideas by himself. Although Whittle's company built the world's first working jet engine in 1937, it was just a prototype and was never used to power an aircraft on an actual flight.

Thanks to the brilliance of its young engineer Hans Pabst von Ohain, Germany was first to build a jet-powered plane. Ohain had earned his doctorate at the University of Göttingen, and by 1936 he began to work for one of Germany's finest airplane designers, Ernst Heinkel (1888–1958). The following year, von Ohain carried out a successful ground test of a jet engine shortly after Whittle's own test and, with Heinkel's support, raced ahead of Whittle's team to put his aircraft into the air first.

Both men were years ahead of their time. Whittle gained backing for his invention only after the outbreak of war, while Germany's leaders were more interested in developing rocket-powered missiles than in von Ohain's work.

How things work

Breaking the Sound Barrier

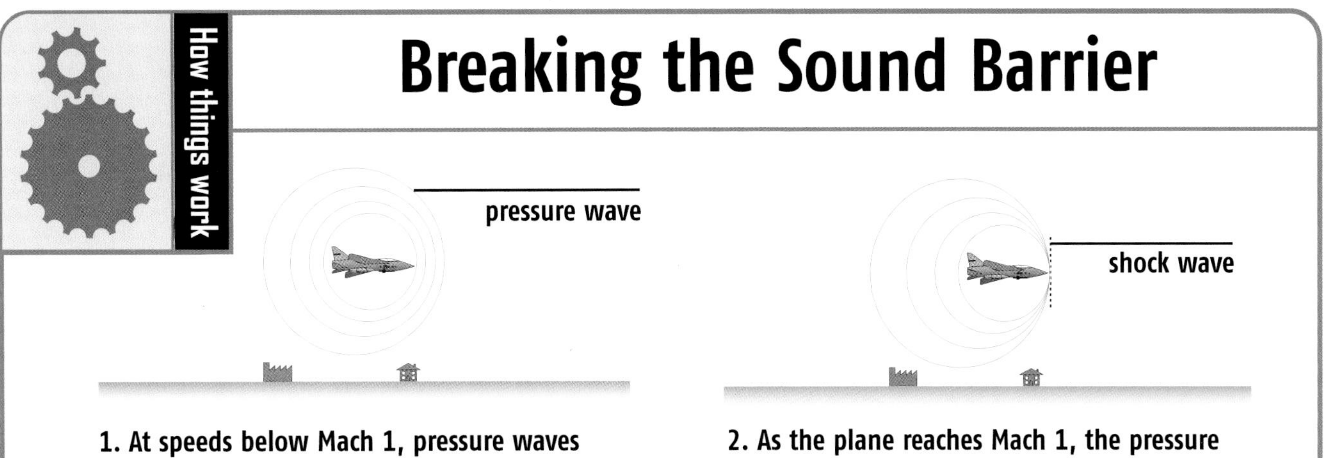

Sound is carried by waves in the air. These waves travel at roughly 760 mph (1,223 km/h) at sea level, but only around 660 mph (1,062 km/h) at 35,000 feet (10.5 km) because of the thinner air and colder temperatures at higher altitudes. The speed of sound is sometimes known as Mach 1, after Austrian physicist Ernst Mach (1838–1916), who did much to advance the study of aerodynamics. Speeds slightly above or below Mach 1 are described as transonic. Aircraft flying faster than the speed of sound are known as supersonic. Mach 2 is twice the speed of sound, and speeds above Mach 5 are described as being hypersonic.

As an airplane travels through the sky, it generates pressure waves in the air that spread out all around it like the ripples on the surface of a pond. When they reach our ears we detect the waves as the noise of the planes. The waves that travel in front prepare the air ahead for the plane, so as the plane reaches this air it has already started to move out of the way and flow around the aircraft.

Ernst Mach was a pioneer in the field of aerodynamics.

At transonic speeds, something different happens. The plane is traveling so fast that it catches up with its own pressure waves. The air ahead has no time to move out of the way, so it simply gets compressed (tightly squeezed) into huge shock waves. These waves can generate a massive amount of turbulence, vibrating the plane and making it hard to control.

At supersonic speeds, the plane travels ahead of its own pressure waves so flight becomes smooth again. However, its shock waves sweep over a huge area behind it. When they reach the ground, people hear them as a deafening "sonic boom" even when the plane is miles away. A sonic boom can even be powerful enough to break windows on the ground!

How things work

Wing Shapes

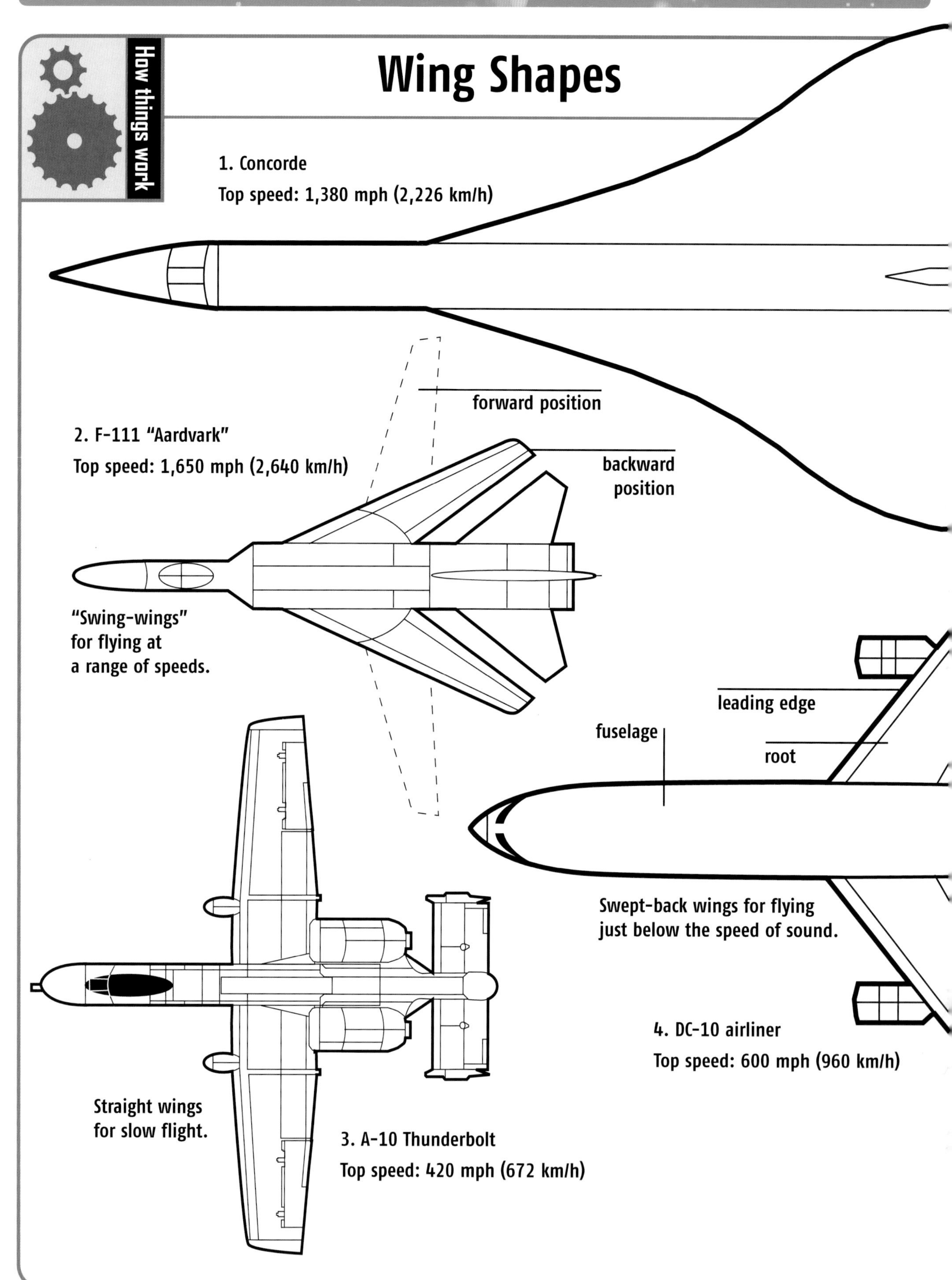

Wing Features

A wing's leading edge is the curved surface at the front of the wing that cuts through the air first. The back of the wing is called the trailing edge. The root is the section of wing that joins to the aircraft's body, or fuselage, and the tip is at the other end. The tips of most wings are slightly higher than the root.

Shape and Speed

A wing's shape affects how fast an aircraft can fly. Aircraft designed to fly at slow speeds have straight wings that stick out at right angles. Aircraft that cruise at speeds just below supersonic, such as airliners, have swept-back wings. Supersonic aircraft have thin, triangular wings—also known as "delta" wings because of the resemblance to the Greek letter Δ. This shape keeps them stable at very high speeds and produces a lot of lift. A few aircraft have "swing-wings," which can switch from a straight to a delta shape so they fly efficiently at all speeds.

tip

trailing edge

Fact **Most airplanes have moveable sections called flaps, slats, and spoilers. The pilot uses them to change the wing shape to help produce more lift or increase drag.**

new jet engines, they opted for a more powerful rocket engine. Launching rockets was still a challenge in those days; launching a rocket-powered plane safely was even more problematic. The Bell engineers decided to carry the *X-1* into the air harnessed to a Boeing B-29 bomber, which would then drop it into midair. This approach would save the fuel ordinarily used during takeoff for a longer high-speed flight.

Many pilots had already lost their lives flying at speeds close to the sound barrier and there was still the problem of finding someone willing to risk his life on such a dangerous mission. One man proved willing to take the challenge. He was Major Charles E. "Chuck" Yeager (born 1923), a World War II flying ace turned test pilot. He climbed into the cockpit on October 14, 1947, and flew into history, shortly afterward, at a speed of 662 mph (1,066 km/h).

The* X-1 *takes off under the power of its own rocket engines for another flight in 1949.

HOW JET ENGINES WORK

A technician checks the fan blades of the huge turbofan engine used to power a Boeing 777. The engine is attached to the underside of the wing. Engines in this position are enclosed in a streamlined casing called a nacelle.

Jet engines do not use a propeller to make thrust. Instead, a jet engine throws a stream of hot gas backward through its exhaust nozzle, and it is this that moves the plane forward. This system of forces is an example of action and reaction: the action of the exhaust moving backward produces an equal and opposite reaction force that moves the airplane forward.

Because of this jet engines are also known as reaction engines. They are totally different from propeller engines, which are much more like those used in cars and trucks. Propeller engines are reciprocating engines, since they produce an up-and-down motion. Reciprocating engines spin wheels or propellers with the downward motion of their pistons. Obviously each piston then needs to be raised up before it can push down again and contribute to the turning of the engine. This upward motion wastes a lot of time and energy, and only a portion of a reciprocating engine's movement actually ends up spinning propellers.

Jet engines do not waste time or power like this. They are gas turbines—engines that burn a continuous stream of fuel and convert the energy released into a spinning motion. Reciprocating engines burn small amounts of fuel in short bursts. In a jet engine, however, fuel and air are constantly moving through the combustion chamber in a powerful stream. This means much more of the energy released ends up driving the airplane forward.

A jet engine has thousands of parts but produces power in only a handful of different stages. Air enters through an inlet at the front. It is then compressed by fan blades (similar to the fan you might use on a hot day) and pushed into a combustion chamber. Fuel is sprayed into the chamber and burns hot in the draft of rushing air. This hot burning mixture turns the blades of a turbine (another fanlike device) at the back of the combustion chamber. The spinning turbine drives the compressor fans and the pumps that squirt in the fuel. Finally, hot gases produced when the fuel is burned shoot back through the jet's exhaust nozzle, providing the thrust.

High-performance engines have afterburners. These spray more fuel into the stream of hot exhaust gases just before they leave the engine. As this extra fuel burns it adds to the overall thrust produced.

How things work

Different Jet Engines

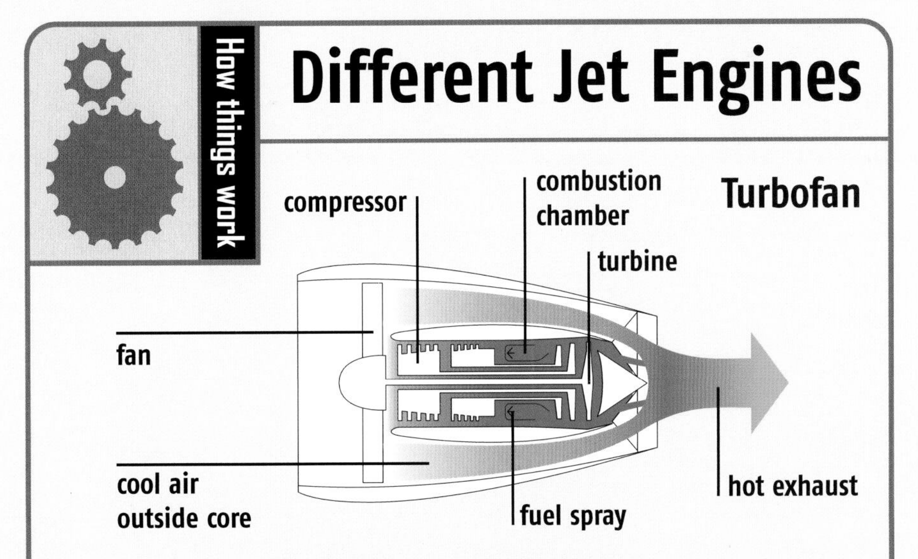

Turbofans and Turbojets

Most aircraft, including passenger airliners, have turbofan jet engines. These have gigantic fans fitted to the front, which drive huge amounts of air into the compressor and combustion chamber. But the fan, which, along with the compressor, is driven by the turbine, also blasts cool air around the outside of the engine core, generating extra thrust. The air sucked in by the engine fan compensates for thin air at high altitudes.

The first jet engines—known as turbojets—did not have this fan. All the air in a turbojet travels through the combustion chamber. Early versions were very inefficient—less than a third of the air taken in was used to burn fuel. Modern turbojets power supersonic airplanes because fans do not work at very high speeds.

Turboprop engines

Turboprop engines use a jet engine in a different way, in this case to turn a conventional propeller. The engine routes most of its power to a drive shaft turning this propeller. The propeller then provides thrust in the same way it does when rotated by a reciprocating engine. Some of the air that is pushed back by the propeller is forced into the combustion chamber increasing the efficiency of the jet section. Turboprops are very efficient engines because the propeller and jet sections work to drive each other.

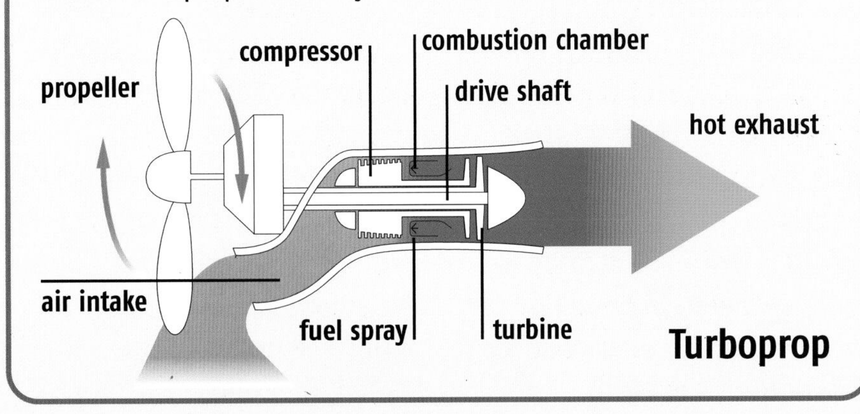

SKY CRUISERS

A Boeing 747 takes off under the power of its four huge turbofan engines. 747s are the largest jet airliners in use today.

During the first decades of the 20th century, airplanes developed at a tremendous rate, and not just in terms of the speed at which they could fly. Zeppelins and other airships had shown just what air travel could achieve, but they often exploded and were too slow to be a practical means of global transportation. In peacetime, more passenger airplanes were developed. These sky cruisers heralded a new age of world travel, with people and freight traveling across oceans and continents faster than ever before.

EARLY DAYS

Early airplanes carried only one or two people, but the need to carry even greater loads soon became apparent. In 1914, U.S. airman Tony Jannus ran the world's first airline service carrying small loads of freight or passengers across Tampa Bay in Florida.

The first regular air service in the United States took to the skies in the 1920s after the U.S. Post Office Department created an airmail service. The mail planes began to carry paying passengers, too, and by the mid-1930s they were carrying passengers and cargos across the world.

THE COMING OF THE JETS

The British Post Office had been using de Havilland airplanes for long journeys around the world, but it was a U.S. airplane that truly ushered in the modern age of air travel in 1933. With a top speed of 180 mph (300 km/h) and a range of 750 miles (1200 km), the Boeing 247 made fast and convenient air travel possible for up to ten passengers. Despite its small capacity, the Boeing 247 is generally considered to be the first real airliner.

The most successful of early airliners was the Douglas DC-3 "Dakota," which entered service in 1936. The Dakota was the most sophisticated and successful plane of its age. Like the Boeing 247, it was an all-metal monoplane with two propeller engines and had a similar top speed of 190 mph (305 km/h). However, the DC-3 carried 21 passengers—more than twice as many as its rival.

These early airliners were developed before jet engines had even been tested, and all passenger planes were driven by propellers until the 1950s. By then the largested airliners had four propeller engines and could carry 100 passengers at speeds of more than 300 mph (480 km/h).

People and society

Is it a Boat? Is it a Plane?

Many of the first long-distance air travelers would have not set off from an airport, but from a dock. This was because they were passengers on a flying boat (above). With a fuselage shaped like the hull of a boat and propellers mounted high up, flying boats were designed to take off and land on stretches of calm water.

Originally invented by Glenn Curtiss in 1912, flying boats really came into their own in the 1930s. They were especially useful for shuttling passengers and freight at a time when few airports had been built. In 1936, flying boats began regular services between Britain and outlying parts of the British Empire, such as South Africa. The seaplanes could only fly for a few hours at a time, and long journeys often took many days. To compensate for their slow speed, most flying boats had luxurious cabins, and the pilots would land at mealtimes.

The most impressive flying boat was the 12-engine German Dornier Do X. This monster could carry 150 passengers in considerable style. The last commercial flying boat, the Sikorsky VS-44A, was introduced in 1942; by the 1950s, flying boats had largely been replaced by airplanes and helicopters.

Key inventions

The de Havilland Comet

Britain pioneered the passenger jet on May 2, 1952, when the de Havilland Comet (above) took to the sky. It was an enormous advance over previous aircraft and traveled at speeds of nearly 500 mph (800 km/h). The first flight was between London, England, and Johannesburg, South Africa.

Air is much thinner at high altitudes, so the Comet had a pressurized cabin to make it easier for the passengers and crew to breathe. In a pressurized cabin, the air is made "thicker" by keeping it at a higher pressure than the air outside. Although its pressurized cabin made travel by Comet something of a luxury, it also led to tragedy. In January and April 1954, two comets were ripped apart in midair, killing everyone onboard. Engineers later discovered that the plane's metal fuselage was too weak to withstand the difference in pressure between the inside of the cabin and the thinner air outside. Later airplanes were built with much stronger fuselages as a result.

By this time, jet engines had become powerful, safe, and efficient enough to be used on planes of this size. The world's first passenger jet, the Comet, made by British company de Havilland, was introduced in 1952.

THE AGE OF THE AIRLINE

Other manufacturers soon followed with jet airplanes of their own. In 1958, the Boeing Company introduced its 707, a four-engine jet that had taken several years to develop. It was immediately put into service by the U.S. airlines. On October 26, 1958, Pan-American World Airways (PanAm) began flying 707s between New York City and Paris, France, and within months American Airlines 707s were carrying passengers between New York and Los Angeles.

Other popular jets of the late 1950s included the Convair 880 and 990 and Douglas DC-8. All of these used turbojet engines similar to those designed by Frank Whittle, who invented jets in the 1930s. Other airplanes, including the Lockheed Electra, opted for turboprop engines that used a propeller and a jet together. Turboprops are more economical than turbojets but cannot be used to fly as fast.

The new jet airliners were used for international travel and other long-distance journeys throughout the 1960s. Smaller planes were developed during this decade for flying shorter distances more economically. These included the Boeing 727 and 737 and the Douglas DC-9.

Voyager (above) is the ultimate long-distance aircraft. In 1986, the plane took nine days to fly 25,000 miles (40,000 km) non-stop around the world. *Voyager* is unique because it did this on just one tank of fuel. Apart from the cockpit, the entire plane, even the wings, was filled with engine fuel.

BIGGER, FARTHER, FASTER

The year 1970 saw the introduction of an airplane bigger than anything anyone had ever seen before, the Boeing 747 or "jumbo" jet. At a time when most jets were still carrying less than 200 people, the first jumbo jets made it possible to transport around 400 people at a time. (The latest version can carry 524 people.) The 747 is 232 feet (71 m) long, roughly the same length as 15 cars, and its wings stretch almost as far from tip to tip. Jumbo jets are not simply big; they can also fly the distance from New York to Tokyo without stopping.

With a top speed of more than 550 mph (885 km/h), they are fast, too. Between October 28 and 30, 1977, a PanAm jumbo set a world speed record for circling the globe (flying over both poles) when it traveled a distance of 26,383 miles (42,450 km) in 54 hours. The combination of high speed and huge capacity, however, make the 747 especially fuel hungry. Although its tanks carry 48,000 gallons (180,000 liters) of fuel, it guzzles more than 3,300 gallons (12,500 liters) an hour!

Airliners also crossed the sound barrier in the 1970s. A joint project between Britain and France developed the world's first supersonic (faster-than-sound) airliner—Concorde. While Concorde was still being tested, the Soviet Union put a similar supersonic plane into service. Its Tupolev (*continued on page 46*)

INSIDE A 747

The Boeing 747 "Jumbo" is one of the largest aircraft in the world, more than ten times the size of Boeing's first airliner, the 247. The historic 120-foot (37-m) flight of the Wright brother's *Flyer* could have taken place inside a 747's cabin. Since 1970, the world's 747s have carried 1.8 billion people 24.7 billion miles (39.5 billion km). An international flight can last many hours, and airlines pack 5 tons (4.5 metric tons) of food for the passengers. About 170 tons (153 metric tons) of luggage can be loaded into the hold inside seven minutes.

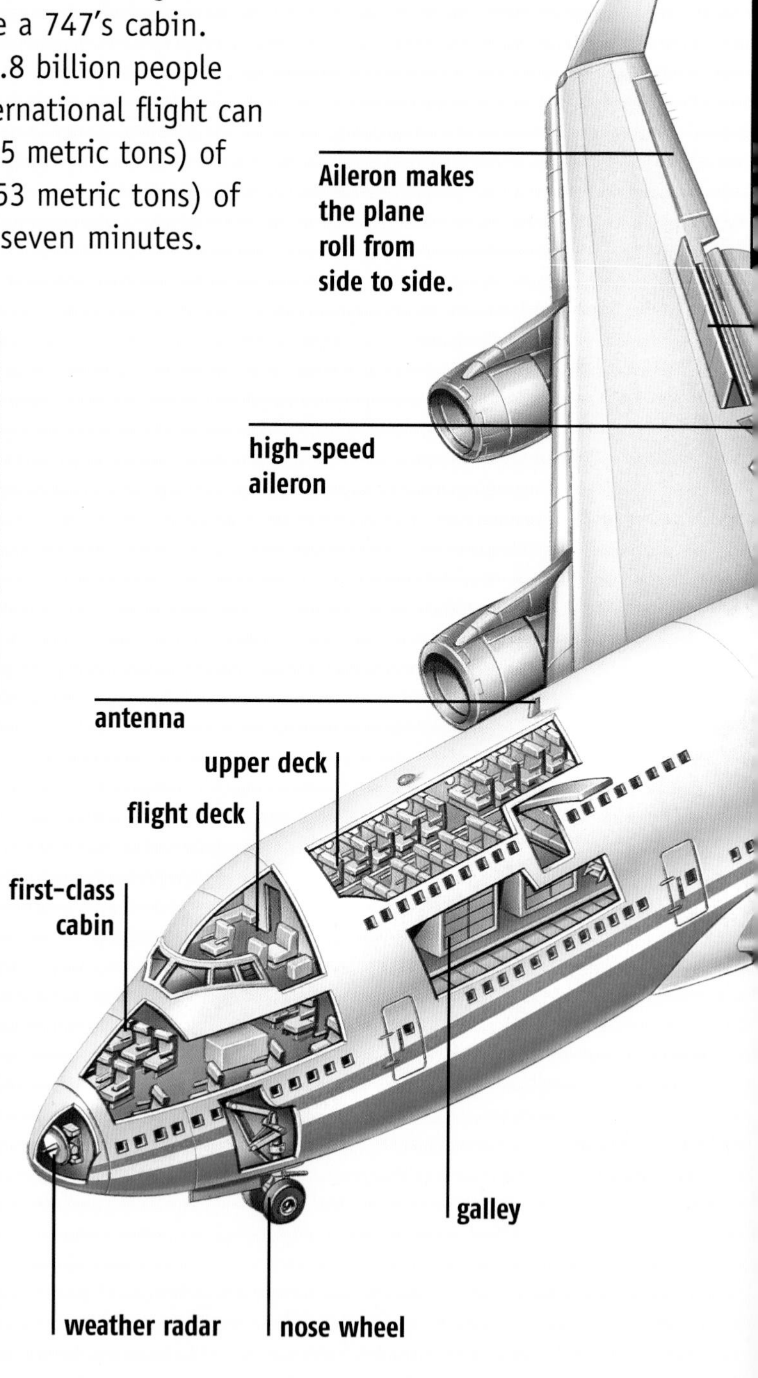

Old and New

The DC-3 Dakota was the jumbo jet of its day. Its 21 passengers sat on two long benches that ran along the cabin walls.

When the giant A380 enters service in 2006, it will carry more passengers and cargo than 747s but use less fuel.

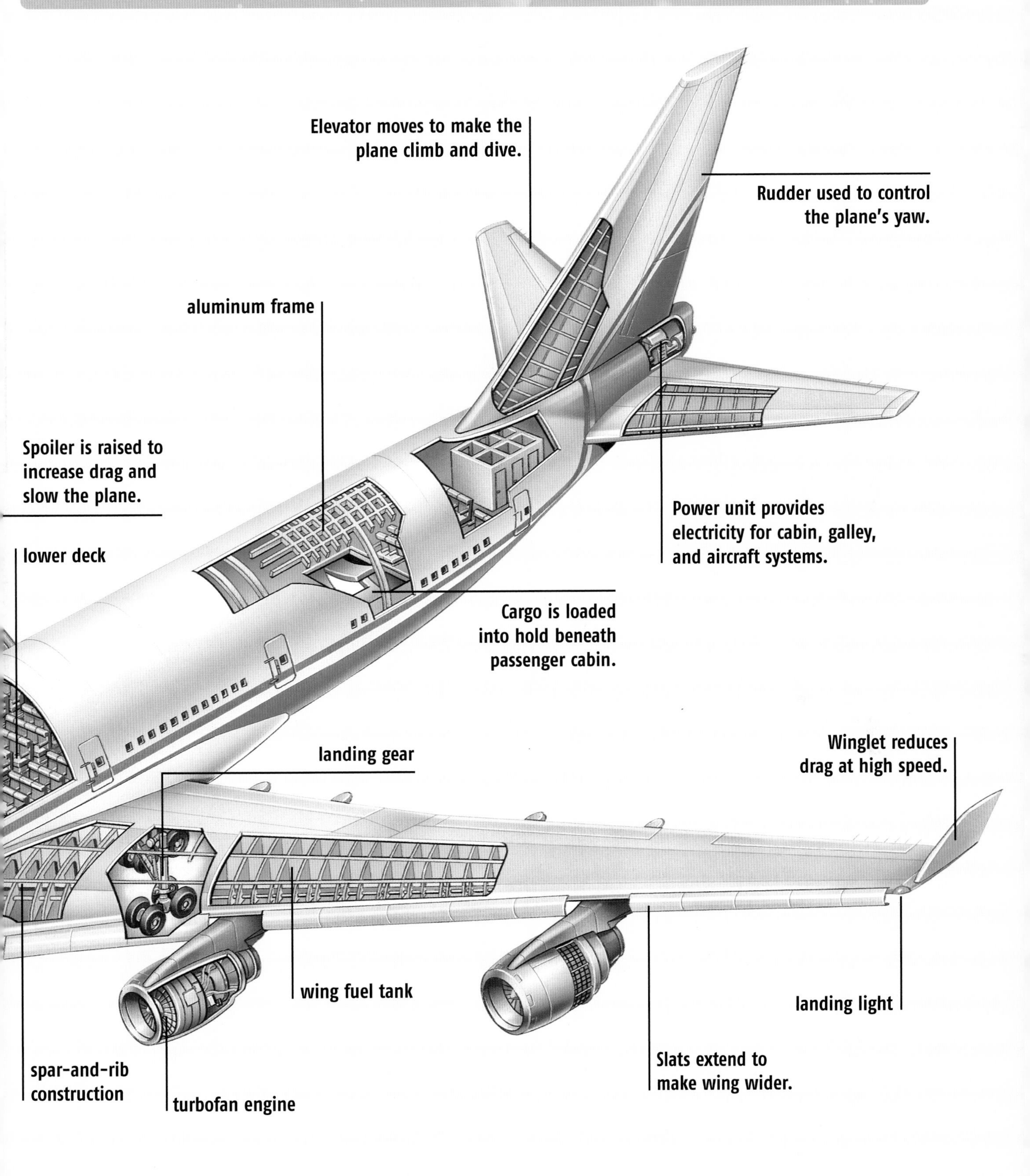
Elevator moves to make the plane climb and dive.
Rudder used to control the plane's yaw.
aluminum frame
Spoiler is raised to increase drag and slow the plane.
lower deck
Power unit provides electricity for cabin, galley, and aircraft systems.
Cargo is loaded into hold beneath passenger cabin.
landing gear
Winglet reduces drag at high speed.
wing fuel tank
landing light
Slats extend to make wing wider.
spar-and-rib construction
turbofan engine

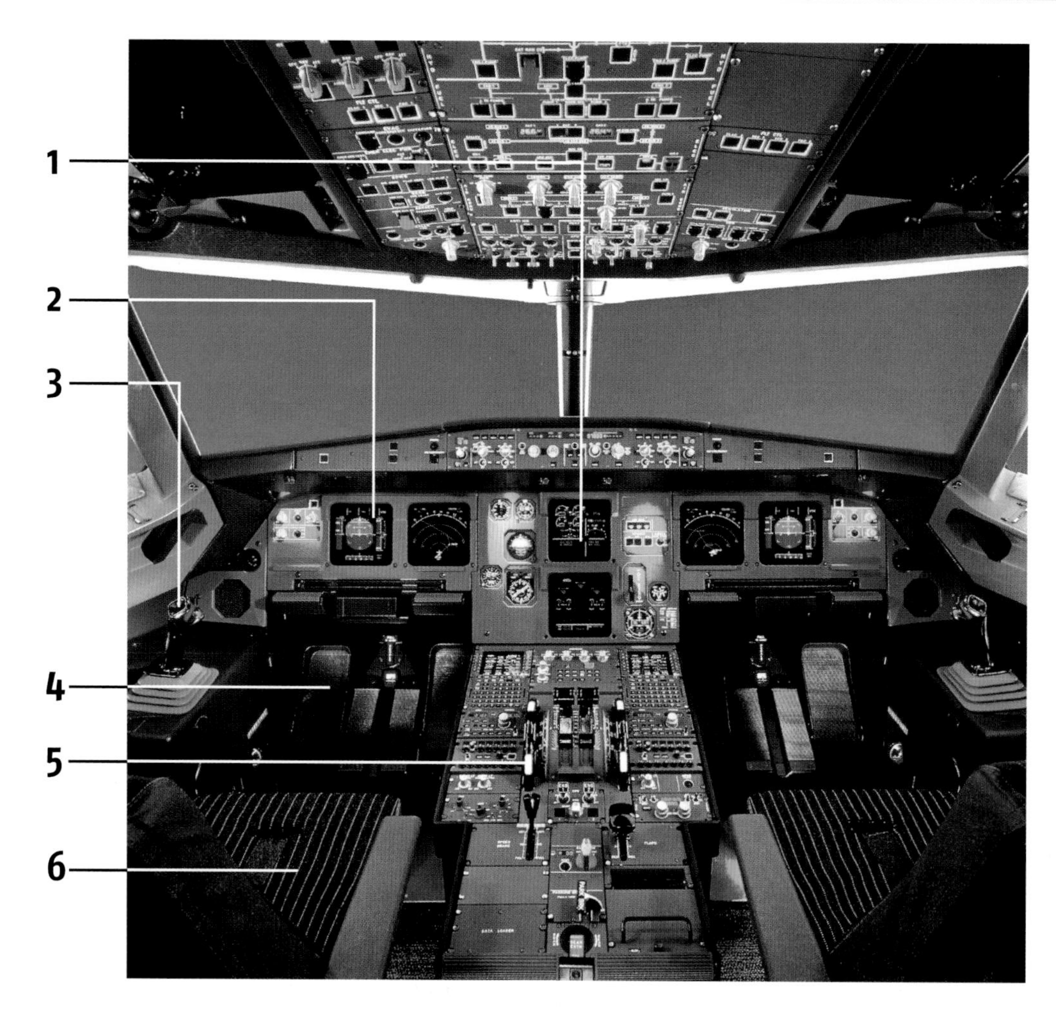

Flight Deck

1. The pilots can find out information about the aircraft, such as how the engines are performing, from these screens.

2. Navigation aids are displayed in front of the pilot to show the position of the aircraft.

3. This control column is linked to a computer. When the pilot moves the column, the computer transmits the information to the control surfaces.

4. The rudder pedals are also linked by computer to the tail rudder.

5. The throttle controls the amount of power provided by each engine.

6. The pilot in charge of the plane always sits in the left seat. The copilot sits on the right.

Tu-144, nicknamed "Konkordski," began cargo flights in 1975, but Concorde was the first to carry paying passengers in 1976. The Tu-144 was withdrawn in 1983 after proving to be unsafe. Concorde continued to be the world's fastest airliner until it was withdrawn from service in 2003.

Jet airplanes have continued to evolve ever since. Nearly all modern airliners are built by just two companies. Boeing have outperformed their other U.S. rivals to become the world's largest aircraft manufacturer. Their "7" range has grown and now includes the 757, 767, and 777. Boeing's largest rival is Airbus, a group of European companies that work together to produce another range of aircraft. Like Boeing's, this range grew from one airplane, the A300, which first flew 1972.

INTO THE FUTURE

No one knows quite what the future holds for the travel industry. NASA engineers are currently developing a new type of supersonic jet airliner that could fly from Los Angeles to Tokyo in just four hours—less than half the time it takes today. With a radical new engine design, the new plane should be much quieter than the supersonic aircraft of today. Less radical but much bigger airplanes are also now in development. The Airbus

A380 will be the widest aircraft in the world. Its two decks will have room for several hundred seats and could even be equipped with private cabins. Boeing plans a rival plane, called the 747X, based on a stretched 747.

Modern airplanes offer a choice between "very fast" and "very large." Concorde could carry only 120 passengers, while the 747 carries four times more. But a 747 flies at only 550 mph and Concorde could achieve 1,350 mph (2,170 km/h), three times as fast. If the passenger airplanes of tomorrow are going to combine "very fast" and "very large," they will need to look very different from those of today.

Some may have curved, C-shaped wings and a gigantic fuselage. Others may have their wings and body merged together to create huge cabins with room for 800 passengers. Another new design does away with the fuselage altogether. Rather like a gigantic boomerang, it has no body at all. Instead, passengers sit inside a huge "maple-seed wing" that spins round and round. Another exciting development could see airliners equipped with rockets to make them into spaceplanes. These would take off and land like conventional planes, but make their journeys in space, just outside Earth's atmosphere, at speeds up to Mach 15.

How things work

Safety on a Modern Plane

Flying has become one of the safest ways to travel; all sorts of safety features on a modern airplane are designed to keep it that way. Inside the cockpit, airplanes have a range of instruments so the pilots can ensure everything is as it should be. Trained pilots can always "fly by instruments," control the plane without being able to see where they are going, so bad weather and flying at night usually present no danger. The best instruments in the world offer no protection against two common hazards, however. Birds often hit aircraft during takeoff and landing and are sometimes sucked right through the engine, causing fires. Another danger is caused by ice forming on the wings at high altitudes. This greatly increases drag and even stalls engines. Many planes have special rubber "boots." These strips of rubber on the front of the wings inflate and break off the ice as it forms.

Whether they need them or not, all airplanes carry safety equipment. Every passenger has a safety belt and an oxygen mask, for example, while life preservers (above left) and life rafts are also stowed in case a plane crashes in the ocean. Military aircraft have ejector seats so pilots can escape and parachute to safety even when their aircraft are badly damaged.

CONCORDE

Concorde's pointed nose and delta wings make it instantly recognizable. The noise from its four turbojet engines also make it hard to miss.

Concorde has been the world's best-known supersonic aircraft for almost 30 years. With a top speed of 1,380 mph (2,226 km/h) —more twice the speed of sound—it can fly from New York to Paris or London in four hours. With the six-hour time difference, people flying from Europe arrive before they have even left!

Breathtaking though it may be, Concorde has had a checkered history almost from the moment when the first test plane emerged from a hanger in 1967. Before it even left the ground, the structure of this plane was tested for 5,000 hours, more than any airplane built before. Concorde did not take off for another two years, in 1969, by which time the Soviet Union had already launched an ill-fated rival plane called the Tupolev Tu-144.

Things seemed to be looking up in 1972 when a dozen airlines had placed orders for Concorde. But oil prices surged in 1973 and those orders were quickly cancelled. The British and French governments who had sponsored the project were suddenly forced to share its staggering $3.5 billion cost.

Although the Tu-144 entered service a year earlier as a cargo transporter,

A Tupolev Tu-144 "Konkordski" on display at an airshow. This plane looked very similar to Concorde but had a poor safety record.

Prototype Concordes are prepared for test flights in 1972. The plane in the middle was the model eventually used. The nose cone could be lowered so the pilots could see the ground during landing.

Concorde became the world's first (and only) supersonic passenger plane when it finally took off on January 21, 1976. On that day, two flights set out to celebrate the joint British–French project. A British Airways Concorde left London for Bahrain in the Persian Gulf; and Air France Concorde flew from Paris to Rio de Janeiro, Brazil.

Concorde was designed to operate between Europe and the United States. Flights between London and Paris in Europe and Washington, D.C. began in May 1976. However, Concorde's supersonic speed makes it extremely noisy and authorities in New York City banned it from flying to their airports. Only after a court battle was it allowed to fly to New York in November 1977.

Even then, the new service did not prove a commercial success. Although Concorde can travel at extraordinary speeds, it can carry only 120 passengers and uses enormous amounts of fuel. It took a lot of money to develop and was now proving just as expensive to fly. By 1979, the companies that built Concorde had lost $1 billion and production was halted. It was originally planned to make 300 of the aircraft, but in the end, only 16 Concordes were built.

Nevertheless, Concorde continued to operate as the world's fastest passenger airplane until July 2000 when one Concorde failed to take off properly, crashed into a hotel near Paris, and killed 113 people. The other Concordes were immediately grounded, and the accident was traced to an exploding tire damaging a fuel tank. Even though modifications were made to prevent the accident happening again, people no longer wanted to pay the high prices to fly in Concorde, and the aircraft was retired from service in 2003.

SPINNING AROUND

The Russian-made Mi-26 Halo is the world's largest mass-produced helicopter. It can lift 20 tons (19.6 metric tons), as much as a military transport aircraft.

Not all flying machines have fixed wings. Helicopters create lift with several spinning blades called a rotor. Just like a wing, rotors must rush through the air to create a lift force. However, unlike fixed wings, which travel down a runway to get into the air, the spinning rotor can create lift while the rest of the aircraft remains stationary. In this way, helicopters can move straight up and down, and even hover in the air when the rotor's lift balances the aircraft's weight. The rotor can also be angled to push the helicopter in any direction.

A helicopter's rotor works in much the same way as an airplane propeller. Its wing-shaped blades create a huge downward draft of air that provides the massive upward lift needed to overcome the force of gravity and raise the helicopter off the ground.

HELICOPTERS IN HISTORY

Aviation pioneers took their inspiration from nature. The earliest flying machines had flapping wings, like a bird. The idea of helicopters probably came from seeds that send themselves through the air by whirling around in the wind. Italian painter Leonardo da Vinci (1452–1519) is widely believed to have designed the first helicopter, but the idea is much older. A Chinese book written in 320 C.E. described a toy called a flying top that had a rotor made of feathers.

Although the toy chopper worked, Leonardo's helicopter would not have gotten off the ground. Engines powerful enough to lift a helicopter were not available until the 18th century. British aristocrat Sir George Cayley (1773–1857) built a helicopter driven by steam in 1843, but it was too heavy to rise more than a few inches for a few seconds.

It was more than half a century later before helicopters got any higher. In the early years of the 20th century, a lightweight gasoline engine helped the Wright brothers transform their unpowered gliders into the world's first self-propelled airplane. The same technology put helicopters into the sky. In 1907, French engineer Louis Bréguet (1880–1955) built a four-rotor helicopter called the *Gyroplane* that could hover more than 2 feet (60 cm) off the ground for about a minute.

Although this early machine and others like it could barely keep aloft, they suggested that helicopters really could stay in the air all by themselves. That point was finally proven in 1916

People and society

The Father of Helicopters

Even as a boy, Russian-born engineer Igor Sikorksy (1889–1972) was obsessed with making things fly. At the age of 12, he built a helicopter powered by a rubber band. After learning of the Wright brothers' pioneering flight, Sikorsky soon became an aviation pioneer in his own right, building the world's first four-engined airplane in 1913. Following the 1917 Russian Revolution, Sikorsky decided to emigrate to the United States, where he founded the Sikorsky Aero Engineering Corporation and built many flying boats. It was there that Sikorsky developed the world's first practical helicopter, the VS-300 (above), which flew in 1939. Sikorsky's next model, the XR-4, made the first cross-country flight from Stratford, CT, to Dayton, OH, in 1942. Twenty-five years later, in 1967, two Sikorsky helicopters made the first transatlantic flight from New York City to France.

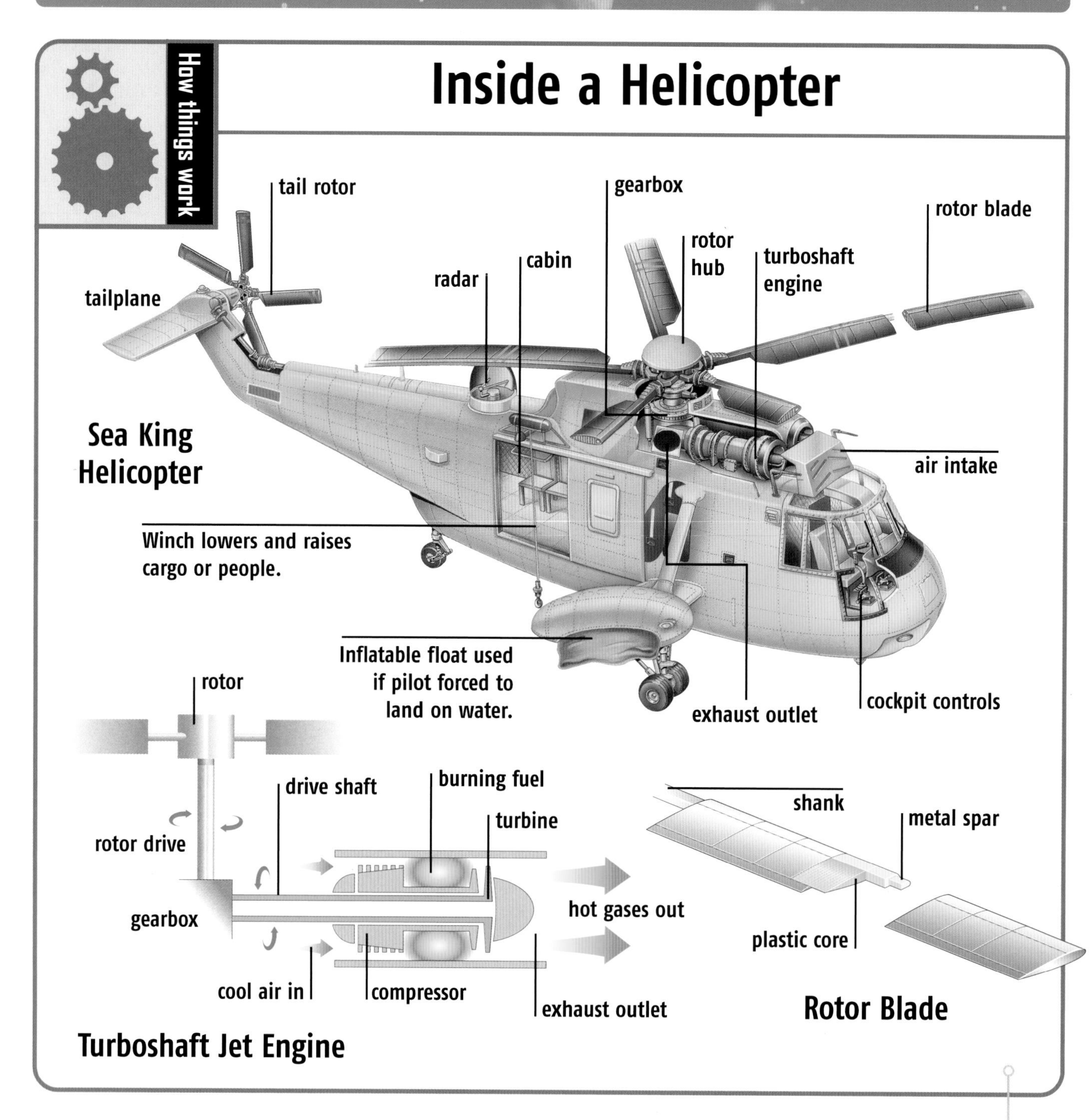

by U.S. physicist Theodore von Karman (1881–1963). He flew his helicopter at a height of 600 feet (183 m) for about an hour.

MODERN HELICOPTERS

An aircraft that combined fixed-wing designs with rotors was invented in 1923 by Spanish engineer Juan de la Cierva (1896–1936). His "autogiros" had rotors instead of wings but were pushed along with propellers. The free-turning rotors spun around as the autogiros moved forward.

Helicopters as we know them today finally took to the skies in the 1930s. A craft called the *Focke-Wulf FW-61*, invented by German aviation pioneer Heinrich

Helicopters are the most versatile of all aircraft, and are not surprisingly very complex machines. Modern choppers are powered by jet engines called turboshafts, which spin the rotor.

Cockpit

A helicopter cockpit has many of the same features found in airplane cockpits. However, the pilot's controls are very different.

1. The pilot uses displays to help him or her fly.

2. The cyclic-pitch control column is used to change direction.

3. The yaw is controlled by foot pedals.

4. The collective-pitch lever makes the chopper rise and fall. Twisting the lever controls the throttle.

5. Unlike in airplanes, pilots sit on the right.

While airplanes have two main controls, helicopters have three. The yaw is controlled by pedals, as in a plane. However, the control column (A) only moves the chopper left, right, forward and backward. The up-and-down motion is controlled by a lever (B) beside the pilot's seat.

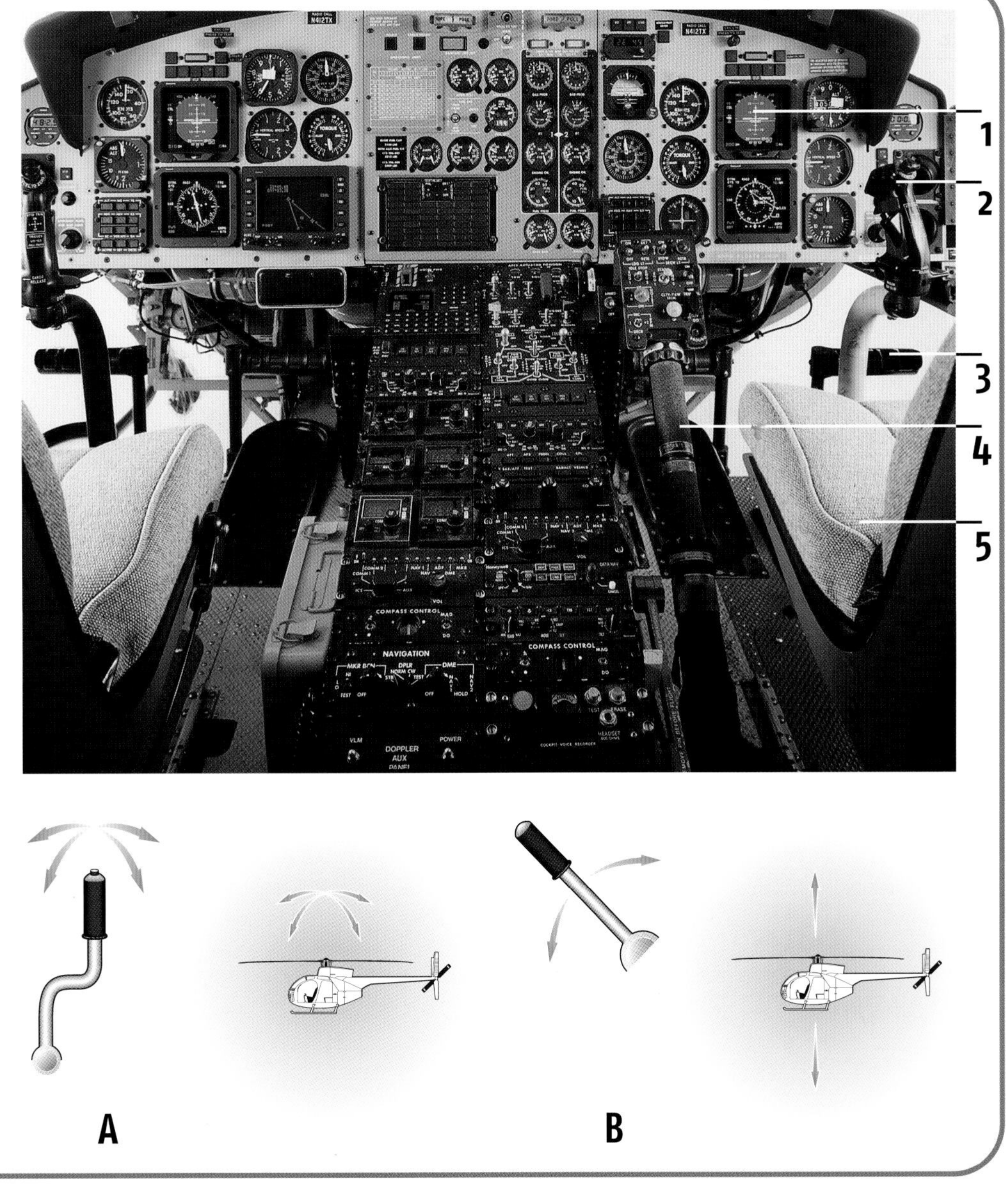

Focke (1890–1979), was the first practical helicopter. Launched in 1936, it set a world record in 1937 by flying to an altitude of 8,000 feet (2,439 m) and staying there for nearly 1.5 hours.

Russian engineer Igor Sikorsky is regarded as the father of the modern helicopter, however. After years of research, he launched the VS-300, in 1939, the first mass-produced helicopter. Sikorsky's VS-300 inspired the design of every chopper now in the sky.

Modern machines include the military Bell AH-1G Huey Cobra, first launched in 1967. This helicopter can lift off at more than 1 mile (1.6 km) a minute and is used by both soldiers and civilians. The most familiar large helicopter is probably the massive troop-carrying Boeing Chinook, with two huge rotors at the front and back. The rotors counter-rotate (spin in opposite directions) and are timed so they never crash into each other.

HELICOPTER STEERING

Without fixed wings, helicopters do not use control surfaces to steer. Instead, they are steered by changing the pitch (angle) of the rotor blades. Rotor blades have an airfoil shape, like a wing. The pitch of a blade has an effect on the lift force it produces. The higher the pitch, the larger the lift force.

During takeoff, the pilot tilts all the rotor blades so they make a very steep angle to the air—have a high pitch. The lift they generate exceeds the weight of the helicopter and it rises up into the air. During landing, the pilot adjusts the rotor so the blades are at a much shallower angle—lower pitch. The lift they generate is now less than the weight of the helicopter, so it lowers smoothly to the ground. When a helicopter hovers, the forces of lift and weight exactly balance one another.

Moving up and down and hovering involves adjusting the rotor so all of its blades have the same pitch. To do this the pilot uses the collective-pitch lever. This lever alters all the blades together (collectively).

The pitch of rotor blades is managed in another way to move the helicopter in different directions. Suppose the rotor blades are altered so they generate more lift when they are behind the helicopter than when they are in front. This makes the back of the helicopter lift up more than the front. In other words, the helicopter tilts and begins to fly forward. If the rotor generates more lift on the left side than on the right, the helicopter tilts and moves toward the right.

To move like this, the pitch of each rotor blade has to change as it swings around the rotor hub, from a shallow angle to a steep one and back again every complete rotation. This cycle of changes is controlled by the cyclic-pitch control column.

As the rotor spins around, the aircraft body tries to spin in the same direction underneath with a twisting force, or torque. The tail rotor produces a force that acts against this twisting force. It is also used to control the helicopter's yaw.

Tail rotor produces the same force as the rotor's torque and so the helicopter faces forward.

The tail rotor produces a force larger than the torque, so the helicopter swings to the left.

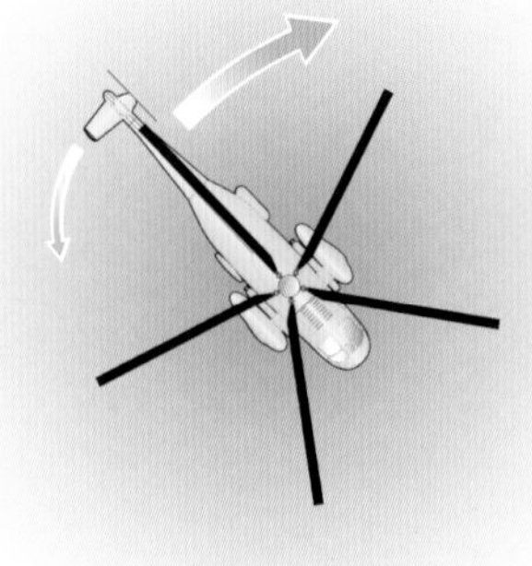

The tail rotor's force is less than the torque so the helicopter swings around to the right.

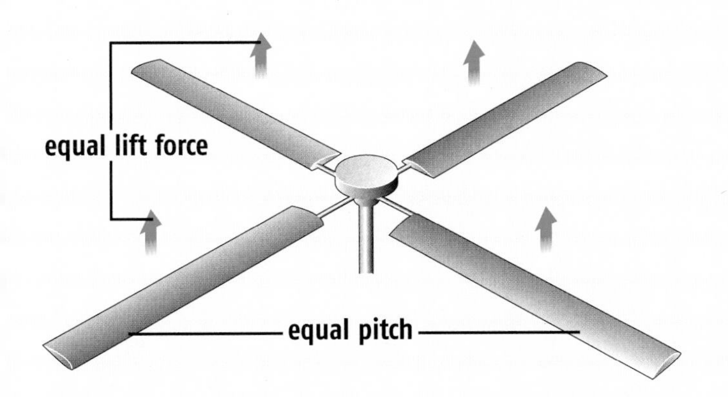

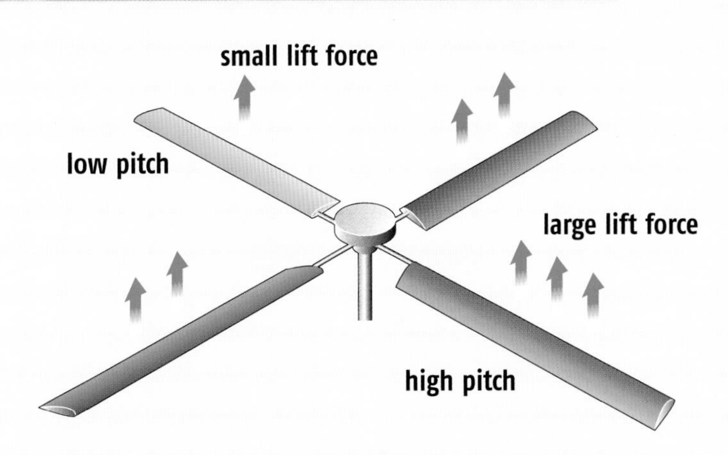

The collective-pitch controls change the angle of each blade by the same amount so they all produce the same lift force as each other.

The cyclic-pitch controls change the angle of each blade individually so they produce different amounts of lift depending on their position.

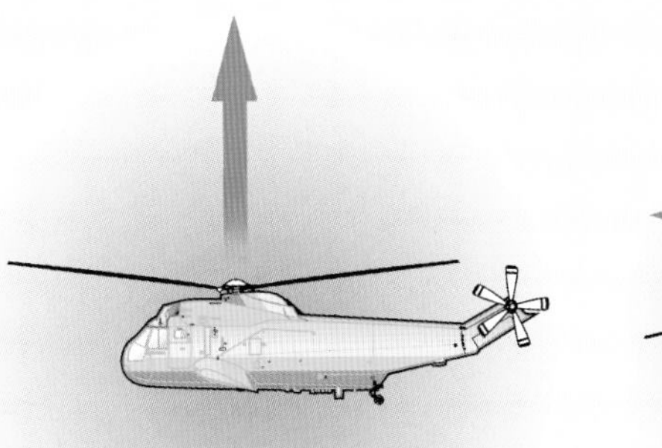

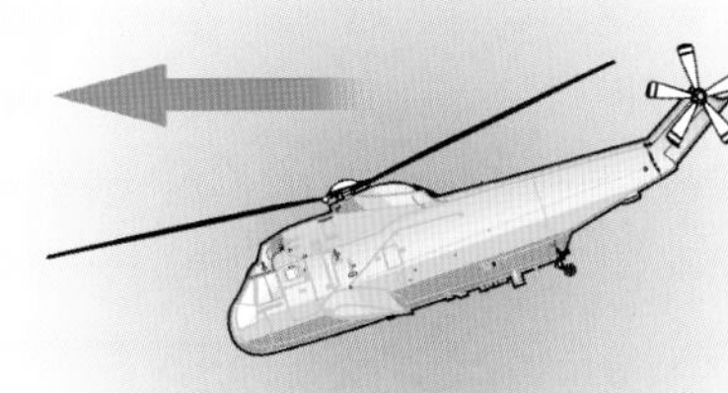

When all the rotor blades have the same pitch, the helicopter moves upward.

When rotors behind the helicopter have the highest pitch, the chopper moves forward.

When rotors on the left of the helicopter have the highest pitch, the chopper moves right.

Drag hinge

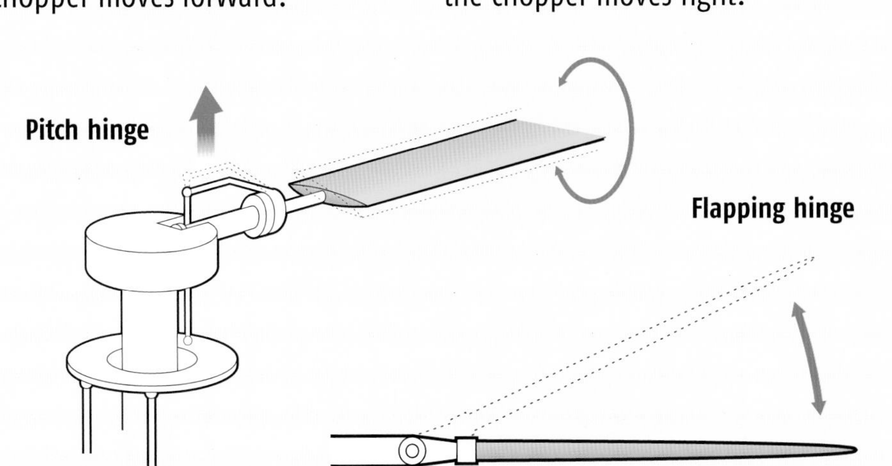

The rotor's drag hinge lets the blade swing back against the drag force as it moves forward.

Each blade's pitch is changed by the pitch hinge inside the rotor hub.

The flapping hinge allows each rotor blade to swing up and down while in flight.

WAR IN THE AIR

An SR-17 Blackbird spyplane, one of the fastest aircraft ever built, flies over California's Sierra Nevada mountains. This plane can fly at the edge of space, and the crew have to wear space suits.

The 20th century's two world wars did much to spur on the development of aircraft. Since the end of World War II in 1945, military needs have led to even faster and more maneuverable airplanes and helicopters. Many of the innovations developed for military reasons, such as jet engines, were used to improve civilian aircraft, too. However, several inventions, like stealth technology, have specifically military purposes.

KOREA: BATTLE OF THE JETS

The jet engine arrived too late to make much of an impact on World War II. In the years that followed, however, most air forces soon built or acquired supersonic jet fighters. These were tested for the first time during the Korean War (1950–1953), a battle between North Korea and South Korea that flared up into a major international conflict. The Chinese, fighting on the North Korean side, had 1,400 airplanes. Half of these were MiG-15 jets built by the Soviet Union (Russia and its neighboring states), which were then the world's best fighter airplanes.

The United States, fighting on the South Korean side, rapidly built a rival fighter, the F-86 Sabre. The air war over Korea soon became a battle between these two formidable jet airplanes. The F-86 triumphed. Only 58 of the

Ejector Seats

Military pilots sometimes need to escape from their aircraft very quickly. They would be injured if they jumped out of the cockpit, so they are ejected clear of their stricken plane.

1. The canopy is blown off by explosive bolts.

2. Small rockets in the pilot's seat blast it out of the plane.

3. Straps pull the pilot's arms and legs in for safety.

4. Once clear of danger, a parachute opens so the pilot can land safely.

U.S. planes were shot down, compared to more than 800 of the Chinese MiGs.

CHOPPERS OVER VIETNAM

Toward the end of the 1950s, the United States once again found itself in another Asian conflict, the Vietnam War, which had raged from 1946 and would continue until 1975. Aircraft played a vital role both in carrying troops and equipment to Vietnam and in the battle itself. Vietnam saw the first use of jets that could fly at Mach 2 (twice the speed of sound or 1,320 mph; 2,112 km/h), such as the Soviet MiG-21 and McDonnell Douglas F-4 Phantom II. Helicopters proved even more important. The U.S. Army used more than 2,000 of them in Vietnam, having turned many of its Bell UH-1 transport choppers —known as Hueys—into "gunships" armed with rocket launchers and machine guns.

TODAY'S PLANES

Some of today's most familiar military aircraft have been in the sky for many years. The huge B-52 Stratofortress bomber first became famous for "carpet bombing"—dropping a large number of bombs over a wide area—during the Vietnam War. A B-52 set a long-distance record during the Persian

No Runway Needed

A Harrier jump jet rises vertically during takeoff. Its downward-pointing jets can be twisted around to point backward when they need to push the aircraft forward.

Military planes often have to operate in places where there are no airports. The United States bases many of its attack aircraft on huge aircraft carriers, which can be used to launch air strikes anywhere in the world. Carrier aircraft are catapulted into the air during takeoff. When landing, the planes grab on to cables that bring them to a halt.

After World War II, warplane designers realized they needed to develop aircraft that could fly as fast as airplanes but that could also take off and land like a helicopter. This led to VSTOL (*V*ertical/*S*hort *T*ake*O*ff and *L*anding) planes, better known as "jump jets." The first plane of this kind was the U.S. Navy's Convair XFY-1, which flew in the early 1950s. It rapidly earned the nickname "pogo stick," because it could take off and land on its tail. A better known VSTOL airplane is the Hawker Harrier jump jet, a British aircraft also used by the U.S. Marines. This has jet engines that point downward, so it can hover in midair, as well as takeoff and land vertically. Another aircraft that needs no runway is the "convertaplane." One example, the Boeing/Bell V-22 Osprey, has large, tilting rotors that convert it from a helicopter to an airplane in mid-air.

Convertaplane: V-22 Osprey

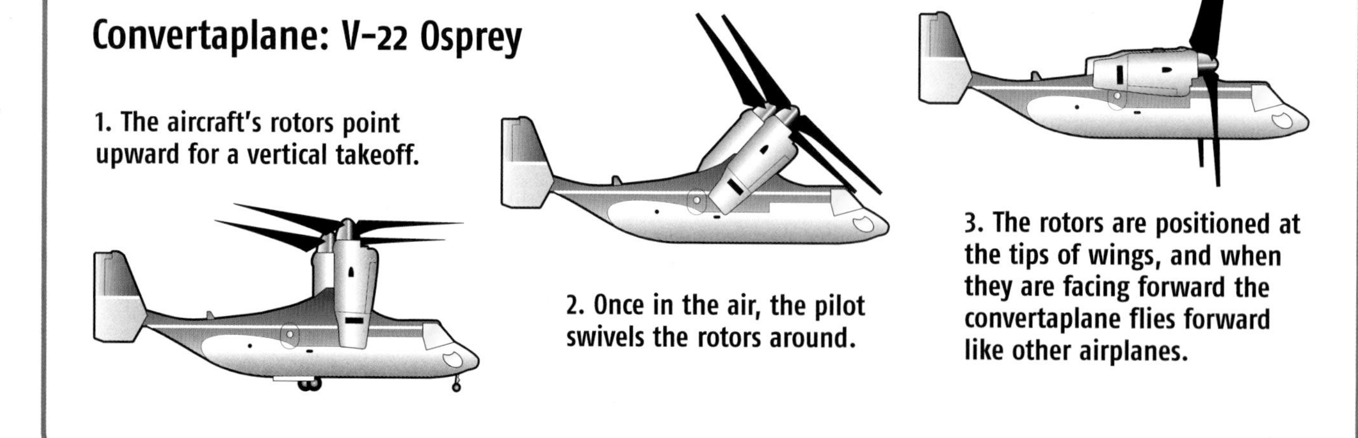

1. The aircraft's rotors point upward for a vertical takeoff.

2. Once in the air, the pilot swivels the rotors around.

3. The rotors are positioned at the tips of wings, and when they are facing forward the convertaplane flies forward like other airplanes.

Gulf War in 1991 with missions that lasted 35 hours, and the bomber is still in use today. Another veteran fighter , the F-4 Phantom, which was launched in 1958, is still used by a few countries, although it was retired by the U.S. Air Force in 1996.

For many years, the world's fastest airplane was the Lockheed SR-71A Blackbird. This famous spyplane had a top speed of more than 2,000 mph (3,200 km/h) and was finally retired in the late 1990s after more than 30 years of service. Other warplanes are used behind the frontline. The huge Lockheed C-5 Galaxy transport plane can carry up to 450 troops and has been a familiar sight in war zones since 1970. Transport helicopters, such as Boeing Chinooks, are used to carry troops closer to the fighting,

Key inventions

Flying Bombs

While unpiloted fighter planes are still a thing of the future, pilotless bombers arrived long ago. They are guided missiles that find their way to a target either by locking on to the heat generated by an enemy airplane or by using sophisticated computer navigation systems. One of the most sophisticated is the Tomahawk cruise missile, a long-range weapon launched from submarines, ships, or dropped from planes (above), which was first used in the Persian Gulf War in 1991.

Cruise missiles can travel a distance of around 1,000 miles (1,600 km) at speeds of up to 550 mph (880 km/h). They fly slower than the speed of sound to avoid detection and sneak through enemy radar by keeping low to the ground. The first cruise missiles could steer themselves to their target using an onboard satellite navigation system. The latest generation (called Tactical Tomahawk) can even be reprogrammed in mid-flight, to go somewhere else as needed.

while attack helicopters are used to spearhead advances. The twin-engined AH-64 Apache, has been a fearsome ground-attack chopper since it went into service in 1982.

Military planes continue to set staggering world records. The world's fastest fighter, the Russian MiG-25, can reach Mach 3.2 (2,110 mph; 3,395 km/h). The best-equipped attack plane is perhaps the U.S. Air Force's AC-130U gunship, which has a range of different cannons and sensors for detecting and defeating enemy targets on the ground. The F-22 Raptor fighter, one of the latest U.S. airplanes, became the world's most expensive military aircraft costing $23 billion to develop.

Another hugely expensive military plane is the U.S. B-2 Spirit, the so-called stealth bomber. Each one costs an astonishing $1.3 billion. Stealth technology was developed in great secrecy by the U.S. military. The idea was to make an aircraft that would be invisible to enemy radar. Instead of having a body shaped

Key inventions

Future Fighters

Military airplanes are always developed in great secrecy, so no one knows exactly what the fighters of the future will look like. A number of airplane companies are currently working to develop a plane known as the Joint Strike Fighter (above). Made from tough but light composites (many different materials combined together), it will be less expensive to manufacture than a traditional metal plane. Engineers at NASA (the U.S. space and aircraft research agency) are using space-age technology to make planes fly faster. One project is trying to develop an aircraft that could fly at Mach 10 (7,200 mph; 11,500 km/h). That would make it more than 200 times faster than the Wright brother's *Flyer*.

Fact

Fighter pilots wear G-suits that help them cope with the huge forces created when they make fast turns. Without the suits, blood would drain from the pilot's head, and he would pass out.

A U.S. Air Force helicopter hovers over a training ground in Nevada, preparing to collect passengers by rope ladder. Helicopters are essential in modern warfare as troop carriers and attack aircraft.

for aerodynamic reasons alone, a stealth plane has a shape defined so that its many surfaces all point in different directions. When a radar beam hits the plane, it is scattered in many different directions or absorbed instead of being reflected back to the enemy in a single beam that they can detect. Stealth planes are also protected against heat-seeking missiles: Its jet nozzles are very wide, so hot exhaust gases spread out quickly when they leave the plane and make less of a target.

NO PILOT NEEDED

Military planes win air battles by being more maneuverable and faster than the enemy. Perhaps the only limit to making deadlier warplanes is the person in the cockpit. A plane can move and turn only so fast without the pilot being injured by the enormous forces involved. Pilotless aircraft that can be flown from the ground by remote control are already used as spyplanes. The U.S. RQ-1 Predator, for example, has been widely used since 1999.

Another advantage of pilotless planes is that they do not have to be large enough to carry a person. A battery-powered U.S. spyplane called Black Widow has a total wingspan of just 6 inches (15 cm) and can be carried in a soldier's backpack. It sends back color pictures from a tiny video camera.

F-117 Nighthawk

The F-117 Nighthawk is another stealth warplane, often referred to as a "stealth fighter."

1. Wide jet exhausts to protect against heat-seeking missiles.

2. Unlike metal, the composite material absorbs radar waves instead of reflecting them.

3. Unlike the curved bodies of most planes, the fuselage is made up of many flat surfaces that reflect radar signals in several directions.

BLAST OFF!

The first rockets were actually fireworks. First used in China, fireworks were powered by gunpowder, a simple explosive. Modern fireworks still work in the same way. The gunpowder is mixed with chemicals that produce bright colors when burned.

Jet engines can take airplanes far beyond the speed of sound, but they can never carry a plane into space. Because they burn a mixture of fuel and air, jet engines are useless outside of the Earth's atmosphere, where there is no air to burn. Traveling in space requires an entirely different kind of engine—the rocket.

ROCKETING INTO HISTORY

No one knows exactly when rockets were invented. Some historians think the Chinese may have been using them in the sixth century, hundreds of years before gunpowder was widely known. Arab merchants returning from China were telling stories about rockets, which they called "Chinese arrows," about 100 years later. Chinese warriors certainly used rockets when besieging a Mongol army in 1232. And it was the Mongols who brought gunpowder and rockets to Europe about a decade after that.

Hundreds of years later still, rockets had been developed into the first long-range missiles. One of the pioneers of military rockets was British army officer William Congreve (1772–1828). Starting from a simple firework, he built rockets that could carry 7-pound (3-kg) warheads over a range of about 2 miles (3.3 km). Like fireworks, Congreve's rockets were guided by long wooden poles.

A V-2 rocket is prepared for launch in 1944. V-2s could carry about a ton of explosive more than 200 miles (320 km).

These rockets were much less accurate than cannons, but the British used them in a few battles during the early 19th century, including against the United States in the War of 1812. (This is how the line about "the rocket's red glare" found its way into the *Star Spangled Banner*.)

Since rockets were not very effective weapons, people began to think of other uses for them. French science-fiction author Jules Verne (1828–1905), wrote stories about space travel, and a Russian schoolteacher named Konstantin Tsiolkovsky (1857–1935) suggested that rockets might be used for this purpose. Tsiolkovsky's ideas about rocket travel were years ahead of their time. He thought up multistage rockets, like the ones that flew to the Moon, and he even sketched out the idea of an orbiting space station. His ideas had a huge influence on U.S. rocket scientist Robert Goddard (1882–1945), who was the first person to use liquid fuels to power a rocket.

ROCKETS OF WAR

It was in Germany that rockets once again became terrifying weapons of war. In 1923, a German physicist called Hermann Oberth (1894–1989) had published an important book called *The Rocket into Interplanetary Space* and went on to lead his own team of rocket designers in the 1930s. Under the Nazis, however, Oberth's work was used not to conquer space but to attack other nations.

In 1942, the Germans introduced their V-1 missile, which used a type of engine known as a pulse jet. Unlike a normal jet engine, which produces continuous thrust, the V-1's pulse jet shot itself forward in a series of short spurts (pulses) roughly 40 times per second. The engine made a noisy buzzing sound as it pulsed on and off and earned it the nickname

Inside a Rocket Engine

From the outside rocket engines look a lot like jet engines, but they work in a very different way. A jet engine takes in air at the front, mixes it with fuel, and throws the hot burning exhaust gases from a nozzle at the back. A rocket engine works more like a gigantic firework. It carries its own supply of fuel (or propellant) on board. But, unlike a jet engine, a rocket engine also carries its own supply of oxygen (the oxidizer) to burn the fuel. This key difference means that a rocket engine can work in outer space where there is no air, while a jet engine would simply grind to a halt if it tried to fly outside Earth's atmosphere. This also explains why a jet engine always needs an opening at the front (to let air in), while rockets generally have a covered nose cone.

Jet engines and rockets do have one important thing in common: they both work by action and reaction. As the hot exhaust gas rushes backward (the action), it pushes a jet plane or rocket forward with the same force (the reaction). A jet engine's power depends on how the air travels through it and reduces as the engine's speed increases; a rocket engine is completely independent of the air around it and has virtually the same power at any speed.

Rocket engines use either solid fuel or liquid fuel. Solid-fueled rockets are little more than gigantic fireworks with a nozzle at the back where the gases escape. Missiles work in this way. Liquid-propelled space rockets are much more complex. The fuel is usually liquid hydrogen and the oxidizer is liquid oxygen. Pumps drive the fuel and the oxidizer from storage tanks, through pipes, to a combustion chamber where they burn at enormously high temperatures.

Liquid-Fueled Rocket

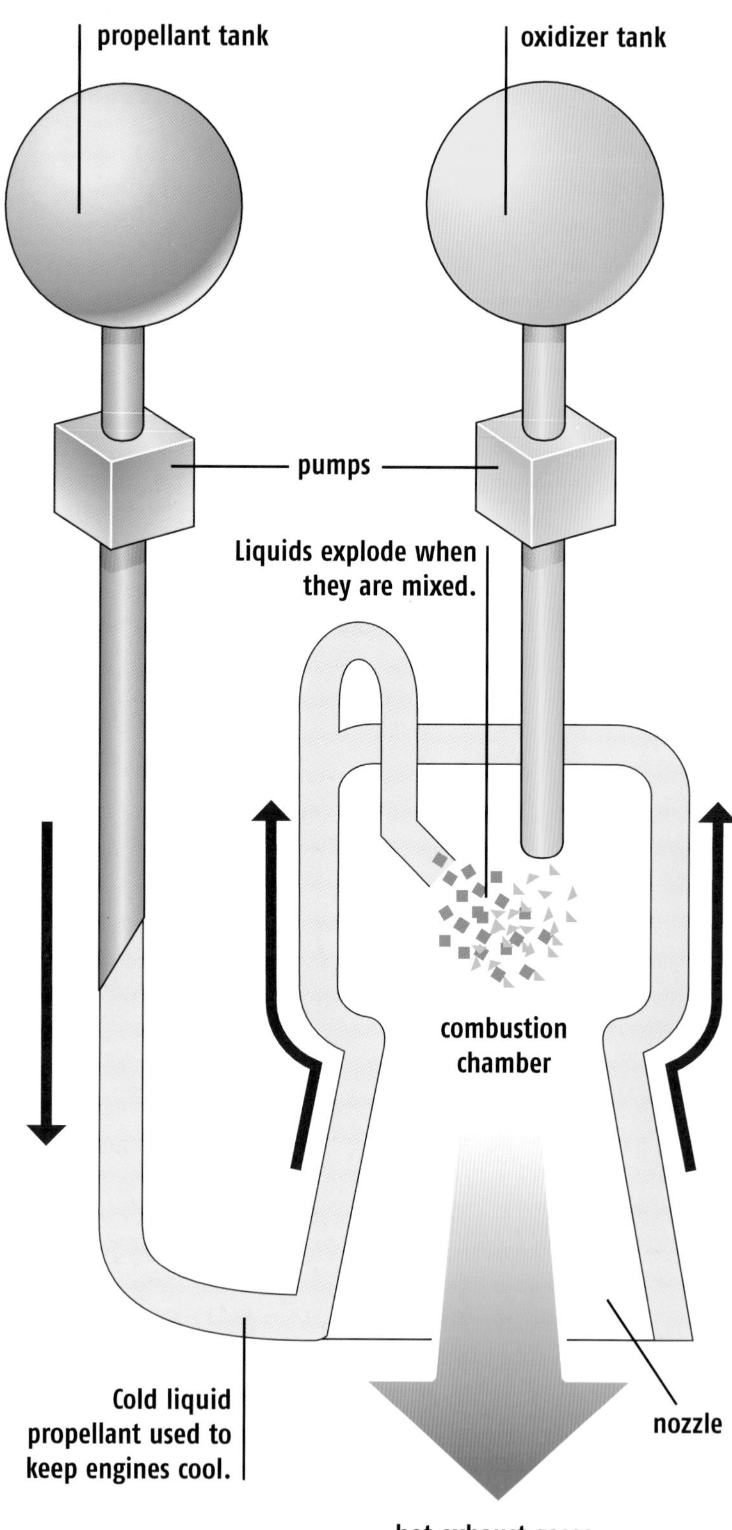

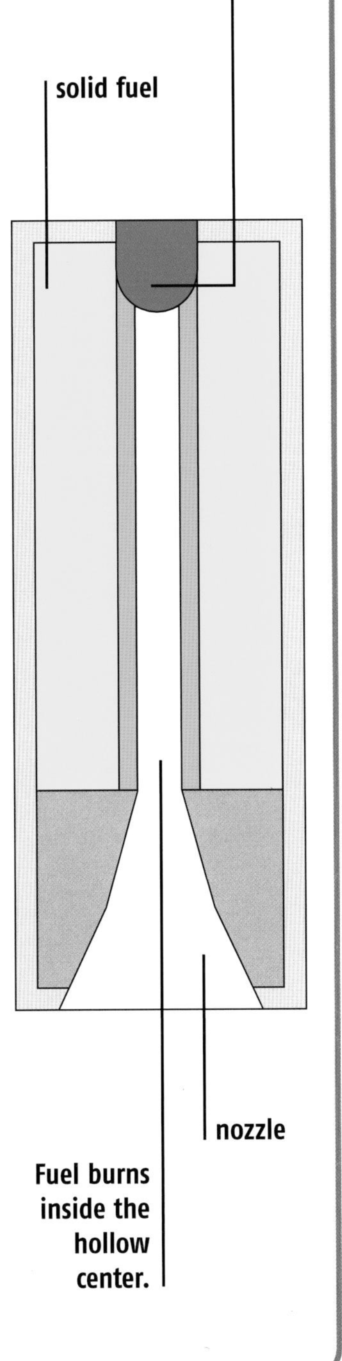

"buzz bomb." These flying bombs, also dubbed "doodlebugs" for their rounded shape, were used in random attacks on civilians.

One of Hermann Oberth's students was a brilliant rocket scientist called Werner von Braun (1912–77). Under von Braun's leadership, the Germans took Goddard's idea of using liquid-fueled rocket engines and tried to improve the V-1. The result was the V-2, a long-range missile that Germany used against its enemies during World War II. The V-2 was a truly terrifying weapon. Because it traveled five times faster than sound, people could not hear these bombs coming until it was already too late to get out of the way. During the war, von Braun and other pioneers battled to produce better rocket-propelled missiles. Once the war was over many of them went to work in the Soviet Union or the United States and turned their attention to traveling into space.

People and society

Rocket Pioneer

Like many other pioneers of space flight, Robert Hutchings Goddard was interested in rockets even as a child. His first step toward space occurred in 1919, publishing *A Method of Reaching Extreme Altitudes*, which suggested rockets might reach the Moon.

Perhaps his greatest breakthrough, however was the discovery in 1926 that rockets flew farther and faster when powered by liquid fuels instead of solid explosives, because liquid fuels released more energy.

Although Goddard (left, with one of his first liquid-fueled engines) worked closely with the U.S. military during both world wars, Goddard's genius was often ridiculed in the press. Only in recent times was Robert Goddard rightly recognized as a great rocket pioneer.

Shuttle astronaut Bruce McCandless flies free in space using the Manned Manuevering Unit jetpack, or "flying armchair."

SPACE RACE

Sputnik *was the first satellite to be launched. It orbited Earth for three months before burning up in the atmosphere.*

Russian spaceman Yuri Gagarin was the first person to travel in space.

World War II accelerated the development of jet airplanes and rockets. When the war came to an end in 1945, an uneasy peace settled on the world. Soon two superpowers—the United States and Soviet Union—were locked in the so-called Cold War, and each side carried on developing faster airplanes and more powerful rockets. The rivalries of this age were played out in all corners of the world and even spilled out into space. Both sides became locked in a "space race," each sending larger rockets farther into space. When U.S. astronauts set foot on the Moon in 1969, the United States became the winners.

THE COLD WAR

During World War II, Germany had been the world's leading developer of rocket power. After the war ended, some of Germany's rocket scientists fled to the Soviet Union. But its leading rocket experts—Walter Dornberger (1895–1980), Wernher von Braun, and 150 of their colleagues—decided to move to the United States instead. In 1945, von Braun became a technical adviser to the U.S. rocket program and began to develop guided missiles for the Americans.

The United States had lagged behind Germany in the war, largely because it had not paid enough attention to the work of its own rocket pioneer Robert Hutchings Goddard. It soon began to catch up, however. In 1947,

People and society

Laika the Space Dog

A female dog called Laika (above) became the first animal in space when she took to the skies in the Soviet *Sputnik 2* spacecraft in November 1957. During the mission, Laika's blood pressure was constantly monitored and details were sent back to Earth by radio. Full details of the flight have never been revealed, however. Official reports stated that Laika survived for a week before her air supply ran out. Other sources claim she died when her cabin overheated a few days into the mission. Animals that went into space after Laika were much luckier. In November 1961, a chimpanzee called Eros orbited Earth twice in a U.S. Mercury spacecraft and returned home unharmed.

Chuck Yeager flew the rocket-propelled plane *X-1* faster than the speed of sound. A more powerful rocket plane, the *X-15*, followed. By the mid-1960s, the *X-15* had reached speeds of 4,500 mph (7240 km/h) and altitudes up to 67 miles (108 km) above Earth. The Space Shuttle flies only about three times higher than this today. The *X-15's* pilots flew on the edge of space and were among the first astronauts.

SPACE SATELLITES

Flying a rocket plane was one thing; launching a spacecraft was quite another. It was not until

1955 that the United States and the Soviet Union announced plans to put satellites (spacecraft that stay in orbit around Earth) into space. Following the end of World War II, the Soviets had developed their rockets in great secrecy. So it came as a huge surprise when they won the first stage of the space race. In October 1957, they put a satellite called *Sputnik* into orbit. People all around the world tuned their radios to listen to the satellite's beeping signal. One month later, *Sputnik 2* carried a dog called Laika into space and proved that living things really could survive beyond Earth's atmosphere and pull of gravity.

Determined not to be outdone, the United States launched its own satellites, *Explorer I*, in January 1958, and *Vanguard I* several weeks later. The U.S. rockets were less powerful than the Soviet ones and their first satellites were very much smaller. Sensing that it was behind in the space race, the United States set up an organization to coordinate its space program: the National Aeronautic and Space Agency (NASA) was born in October 1958.

How things work

How Orbits Work

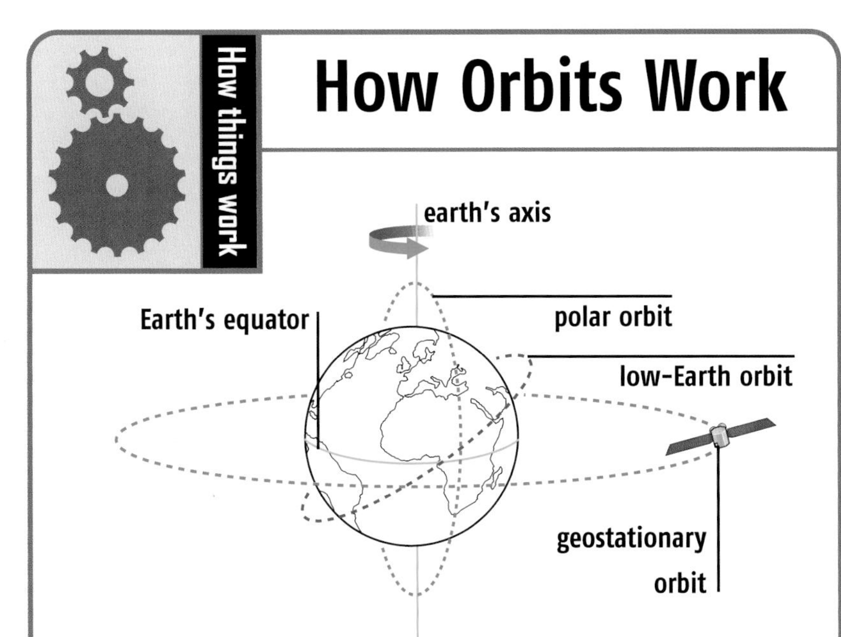

If you swing a ball on the end of a piece of string around your head, it will orbit your body. The string provides the force that keeps the ball from flying off in a straight line.

The planets follow orbits around the Sun. No cosmic string keeps them in place, however. Instead, the force of gravity between each planet and the Sun keeps them in orbit. Spacecraft orbit Earth in the same way. Although many follow an oval path, or ellipse, satellites also follow three different kinds of circular orbits. In a low-earth orbit, a spacecraft travels 190 to 250 miles (300 to 400 km) up in the sky and circles the globe in about 90 minutes. A geostationary orbit is about 100 times farther out than a low-Earth orbit and keeps a satellite in the same place over Earth all the time. Communication satellites move in geostationary orbits. In a polar orbit, a spacecraft travels at right angles to the direction of Earth's spin, and the planet moves underneath it as it orbits. Spy satellites are placed in polar orbits so they can monitor every point on the surface of Earth.

SPACEMEN

Laika, the Soviet space dog, had proved that animals could live in space, but it was not for several years afterward that people would do the same thing. Once again, the Soviets seemed to be racing ahead when they put the first person, Yuri Gagarin (1938–68), into space in April 1961. Flying in a craft called *Vostok I*, he made a single orbit of Earth that lasted nearly two hours before landing safely in Russia. The following month, U.S. astronaut Alan B. Shepherd (1923–98) became the first American in space when he made a 15-minute flight in a Mercury spacecraft.

Giant Steps

If astronauts stepped right out into space, they would die immediately. There is no air to breathe, temperatures can range from an ultra chilly -250°F (-157°C) to a sweltering 250°F (120°C), and the pressure in space is so low that a person's blood would literally boil! A spacesuit's job is to provide a safe, artificial environment in which astronauts can live and work.

The astronauts that went to the Moon wore spacesuits that had no fewer than 24 different layers. The innermost layers were made of soft materials such as nylon and included tubes of water to keep the suit cool. In the middle were layers of neoprene (wetsuit material) to keep the astronauts' blood pressure at normal levels. After that came several alternate layers of aluminum-covered Mylar (polyester film) and Dacron (polyester fiber) to keep the astronauts warm. The familiar white layer on the outside was made of Teflon (the nonstick material also used in frying pans). Not only flameproof, this also protected the astronauts' suits from damage by tiny particles called micrometeorites. The gold-plated visor on the astronauts' helmets protected their eyes from space radiation.

1

2

3

4

Spacesuits

1. The primary life-support unit is carried on the back and supplies the astronaut with oxygen and controls the pressure and temperature inside the suit.

2. The lunar module and astronaut taking this photo are reflected in the tinted visor.

3. The astronaut can alter the conditions in his suit using the controls on his chest.

4. Comfortable "moon boots" became fashionable footwear back on Earth in the 1970s.

Fact The spacesuits worn by Shuttle astronauts are almost twice as heavy as those used on the surface of the Moon, but they are used in the weightlessness of space.

The Saturn V rockets used to fly to the Moon were 363 feet (111 m) high and carried 3,000 tons (2,700 metric tons)

THE RACE TO THE MOON

Robert Hutchings Goddard was ridiculed, in 1919, when he suggested that rockets would one day carry people to the Moon. Forty years later, no one was laughing. In 1961, President John F. Kennedy (1917–63) announced in a speech that the United States would land a man on the Moon and bring him safely back to Earth before the end of the decade. Kennedy realized it was a tough goal, saying: "We choose to go to the Moon not because it is easy but because it is hard."

Throughout the 1960s, the United States and the Soviet Union were battling for the lead in the space race. The United States put a number of astronauts into space with its Mercury and Gemini programs, while the Soviets flew missions in their Vostok and Voskhod spacecraft. By 1964, the Soviets seemed to be winning: their cosmonauts (the Russian word for astronauts) had spent 455 hours in space—nine times as much as the Americans.

Under NASA, the U.S. space program was much better organized than the Soviet one. It also had a very clear goal: to reach the Moon. Both the United States and the Soviets had tried to land space probes on the Moon in 1958. (Probes are craft with no pilot.) The following year, the Soviet space probe *Luna 2* took photographs of the far side of the Moon. The Americans went one better in 1964 when the *Ranger 6* space probe sent back thousands of television pictures of the Moon before crashing into it. It was the Soviets who landed the first space probe, *Luna 9*, on the Moon in 1966, though the Americans arrived only months later with *Surveyor I*. This and other Surveyor missions sent back more photographs and information about the Moon's soil. These uncrewed missions, both Soviet and American, played a vital role in NASA putting men on the Moon in 1969. The Soviets abandoned their moon program in 1972.

MISSION TO THE MOON

"It's one small step for a man; one giant leap for mankind." These were the words spoken by U.S. astronaut Neil Armstrong (born 1930) when he became the first person to walk on the Moon on July 20, 1969. Although Armstrong and fellow astronaut Edwin "Buzz" Aldrin (born 1930) spent just over 21.5 hours on the Moon, it had taken the best part of a decade to get them there.

Project Apollo had been launched by President Kennedy in 1961 with the goal of putting a person on the Moon. The Apollo spacecraft had two major parts: a command and service module (CSM) and a lunar module (LM). These would take off joined together but split apart in space. The lunar module was for landing on the Moon's surface, while the command and service module would provide the power and control to get the lunar module to the Moon and bring it safely back to Earth. The spacecraft was shot into space by a gigantic Saturn V rocket. Designed by Werner von Braun at NASA, it was one of the biggest rockets ever built.

It all sounded straightforward in theory, but there had been a number of major setbacks during the Apollo program. Although the various parts of the Apollo spacecraft were thoroughly tested throughout the mid- and late-1960s, no one knew quite what would happen until the mission was launched for real.

Buzz Aldrin climbs down the ladder of the Apollo 11 lunar module. He and Neil Armstrong spent their moon walk taking photographs and doing experiments.

Lunar Rover

The later Apollo missions took more than just astronauts to the moon. They also carried battery-powered lunar rovers.

1. Astronauts controlled the lunar rover with a T-bar between the seats.

2. The tires were not made of rubber, but zinc and steel wires.

3. The chassis and wheels folded up so the rover could be stored under the lunar module.

Mission to the Moon

The historic Apollo 11 mission to the Moon left Earth on July 16, 1969. The mission took nine days and involved several phases:

1. Saturn V blasts off with the three crew strapped into the CSM. The rocket's first two stages are used to put the spacecraft into orbit around Earth. The used stages fall away and burn up.
2. The rocket's third stage shoots the Apollo spacecraft out of Earth orbit and toward the moon.
3. The Apollo modules separate from the remains of Saturn V. The crew have to rotate the CSM in space to dock with the LM stowed underneath it. They use gas thrusters to steer the spacecraft.
4. The Apollo spacecraft is swung around again and goes into orbit around the Moon.
5. On July 20, the LM and CSM separate. The LM, carrying Armstrong and Aldrin, prepares to land on the Moon. The CSM stays in orbit up above piloted by astronaut Michael Collins (born 1930).
6. The LM lands on the Moon on July 20 in a place called the Sea of Tranquility. A few hours later, the astronauts step from the LM and spend about two hours on the Moon's surface.
7. About 21.5 hours later, the LM takes off from the Moon and rejoins the CSM. Armstrong and Aldrin climbed back inside the CSM. The LM is discarded, and the CSM heads back toward Earth.
8. On the approach to Earth, the command module containing the astronauts separates from the service module and splashes down safely in the Pacific Ocean near Hawaii on July 24.

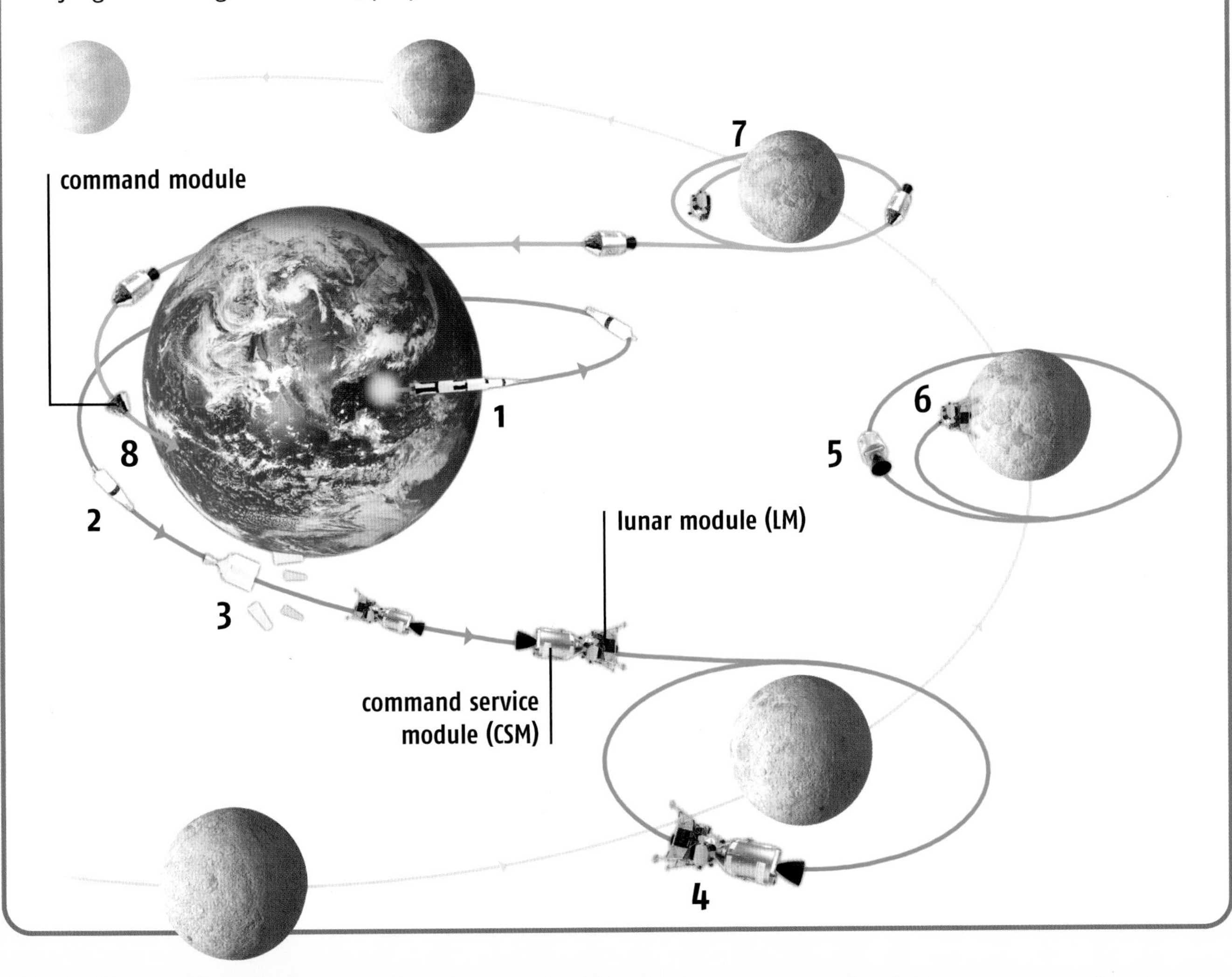

UNCREWED VESSELS

The Hubble Space Telescope (HST) is a large satellite that can see farther into space than any surface telescope. Because it is outside of the atmosphere, HST's large reflecting telescope can make very clear images.

The 1969 Apollo mission is famous as the first space voyage to take people to another world and bring them back again safely. Not all spacecraft carry a crew, however. While satellites spin in orbits around Earth, space probes blaze trails to the far reaches of the galaxy. Controlled by onboard computers and people back on Earth, uncrewed vessels not only help us understand our own planet, they are also the only way to explore deep space.

FROM SPUTNIK TO SKYLAB

A satellite is anything that stays in orbit around a planet or star. Artificial satellites are the stuff of the space age, yet many satellites are as old as the solar system itself. Earth has its own natural satellite, the Moon, while other planets have several of their own.

The modern age of the satellite began in 1945 when British scientist and writer Arthur C. Clarke (born 1917) described the idea of the geostationary orbit. In these orbits, the satellites move at the same speed as Earth rotates, so the satellite stays in the same spot above Earth all the time.

The world's first satellites, the Soviet *Sputnik* and the U.S. *Explorer*, were launched in the late 1950s using rockets based on modified long-range missiles. The first weather satellite, *Tiros 1*, reached space in 1960. Two years later, Arthur C. Clarke's vision became a reality with the launch of the *Telstar 1* communications satellite into a geostationary orbit. This satellite bounced television pictures from one side of Earth to the other, and allowed Europeans to see live pictures

Key inventions

Inside a Satellite

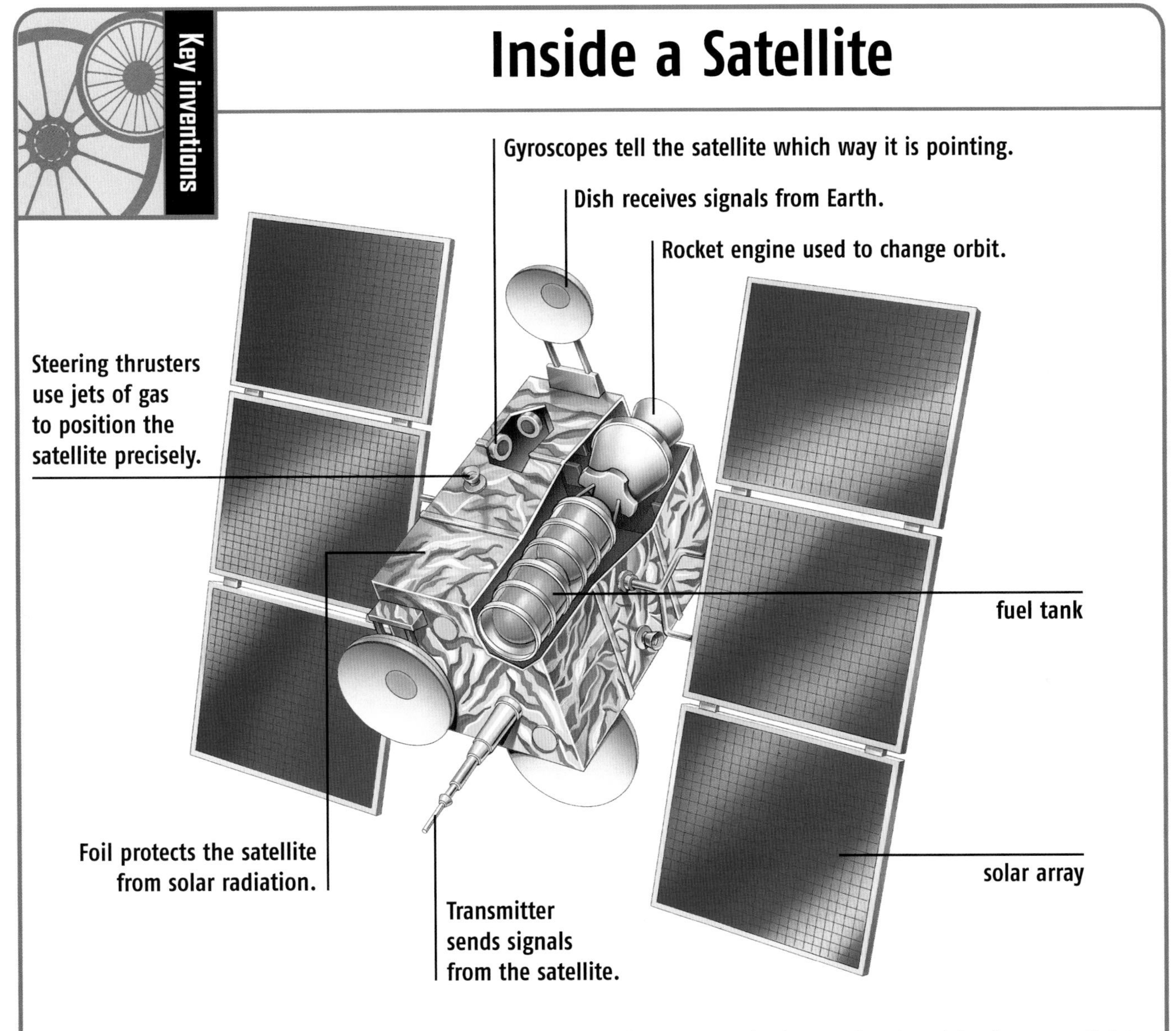

Satellites are made from strong and lightweight metals such as titanium and aluminum so they can be launched as cheaply as possible. Although they are very complex machines, they really need only three main components: the scientific or communications equipment they need to do their job in space, a source of power to use while they are there, and a dish or antenna that can send and receive information between the satellite and Earth. Most satellites are powered by large arrays of solar panels that make electricity from sunlight. Small electric motors constantly reposition the panels so they are always facing the Sun. Satellites are usually launched from rockets, although some have been taken into space—and brought back—by a Space Shuttle. Many satellites also have a small rocket engine and fuel tank so they can move themselves around into the correct orbit, but it takes a much more powerful rocket than this to get them into space to start with.

One of the first images sent back by the **Viking 2** *probe from the surface of Mars in 1976. NASA scientists used the U.S. flag and color charts on the probe to make sure that the image's color was correct. They were amazed to discover that the Martian atmosphere was turned red by tiny dust particles.*

transmitted across the Atlantic from North America. Since then, hundreds of satellites have been placed into orbit around Earth, although not all of them have been uncrewed. Crewed space stations such as *Skylab* and *Mir* are also a type of satellite.

SATELLITES TODAY

Of all modern inventions, satellites are among those that we take most for granted. Most of them are used either for communication or monitoring Earth's surface. Communications satellites (known as comsats) sit in geostationary orbits 22,300 miles (35,900 km) above the equator. Effectively, they work like relay stations in space: They receive live pictures and telephone calls from one place on Earth and transmit them back down to another place in a matter of seconds.

Monitoring satellites, such as those used by weather forecasters, photograph Earth or measure the atmosphere or surface by a process called remote sensing. These satellites stay much closer to Earth than comsats. Usually they follow orbits over the poles about 155–621 miles (250–1,000 km) up that carry them over every point on Earth once a day.

Pioneer and Voyager

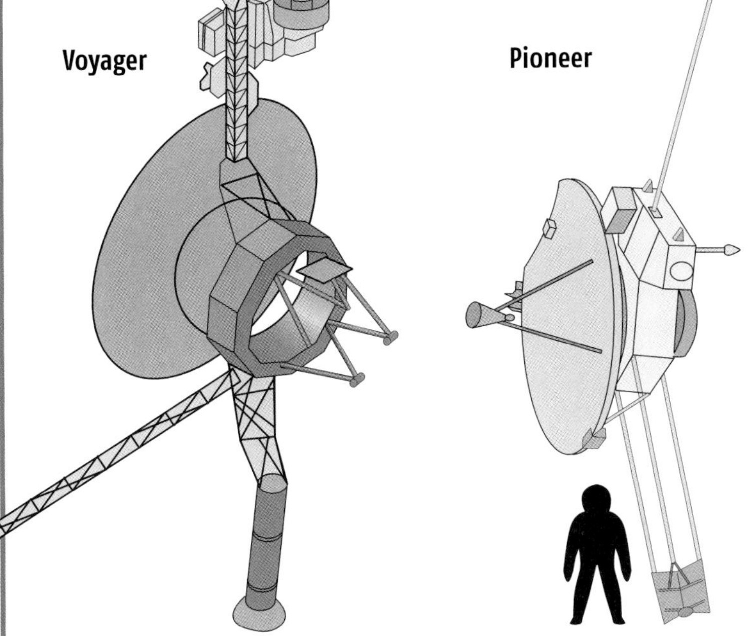

The Pioneer and Voyager space programs explored most of the Solar System's outer planets. Both were designed to probe the space beyond Mars—more than 142 million miles (228 million km) away from the Sun. At this distance, sunlight is too weak to power the solar panels often used by probes and satellites. Instead, the Pioneer and Voyager probes were powered by very small onboard nuclear reactors.

Both programs were a great success. Launched in 1972, *Pioneer 10* became the first probe to study Jupiter in 1973. The following year, *Pioneer 11* passed Jupiter on its way to send back pictures of Saturn and its famous rings. Several years later, NASA launched the much more sophisticated Voyager probes. Packed with scientific instruments and close-up cameras, they sent back many stunning color photographs of the things they encountered. *Voyager 1* reached Jupiter in 1979, while *Voyager 2* visited Jupiter, Saturn, Uranus, and arrived at Neptune in 1989.

Space probes never quite know when to give up. In 1983, *Pioneer 10* became the first space probe to venture beyond all the known planets. Scientists last communicated with it on its 30th birthday in January 22, 2003. By this time, it was about 7.6 billion miles (12.2 billion km) away. The weak signal, thought to be the last from the probe, took more than a day to reach NASA. All four probes are still flying in deep space forever, and may outlast even the Earth.

Although satellites seem remote and mysterious, some are quite well known. For example, the 24 U.S. Navstar satellites provide a service called Global Positioning System (GPS) that allows people to find their position on Earth to within a few feet. *Landsat* takes detailed photographs of Earth's surface and has been used both for scientific studies and for monitoring troop positions during wars. *Inmarsat* is a comsat that people use to make satellite phone, fax, and Internet calls while they are on the move in cruise ships and airliners.

SPACE EXPLORERS

Space probes are built and launched in much the same way as satellites, and the difference between them is sometimes hard to see. A space probe is generally designed to go on a journey of exploration to distant parts of the solar system, while a satellite always stays in orbit around Earth for many years.

During the late 1950s and 1960s, both the Soviet Union and United States launched a number of space probes. One of the first satellites, *Explorer 1*, was also a simple space probe: It carried a detector for measuring radiation in space. In 1959, the Soviet *Luna 1* became the first space probe to leave Earth orbit, flying past the Moon, and then orbited the Sun.

Astronomers had previously had to make do with telescopes, but in the 1960s and 1970s they began to observe the universe through the "eyes" of space probes. *Mariner 2* became the first probe to visit another planet in 1962 when it flew past Venus. Packed with scientific instruments, it discovered that Venus was a forbidding planet surrounded by thick clouds with a surface temperature of around 750°F (400°C). Five years later, a Soviet probe called *Venera 4* made the first landing on Venus. Space probes that land on planets make either "soft" or "hard" landings. Soft landers used rocket engines to touch down gently on the surface, while hard landers hit the ground without slowing down. Some hard landers are designed to penetrate deep into the surface of the planet as they land.

During the 1970s and 1980s, space probes visited a number of other planets. Mariner craft visited Mars, Venus, and Mercury; Viking craft made landings on Mars; the Pioneer missions explored Jupiter and Saturn; and the Voyager space probes visited Jupiter, Saturn, Uranus, and Neptune.

More recent space probes have provided more information about all the planets except Pluto. Many probes went into orbit around the planets, for months or years at a time. NASA's *Magellan* space probe orbited Venus for three years after its launch in 1990. The *Galileo* spacecraft was a two-part probe. After arriving at Jupiter in 1995, it split apart into a satellite that orbited the planet sending back pictures, and a probe that flew into Jupiter's atmosphere to study it close up. *Cassini,* another two-part probe will study Saturn and its largest moon, Titan, when it arrives there in 2004.

NASA's **Sojourner** *rover is prepared by technicians before being launched into space aboard the* **Mars Pathfinder** *probe in 1996. Two days after landing on the planet in 1997, the six-wheeled rover rolled out of the probe onto the surface. The rover analyzed the soil under radio control from Earth. It took 10 minutes for each command to reach the robot.*

Key Inventions

Getting NEAR to Eros

Space probes often become satellites themselves, going into orbit around things so they can study them more closely. In February 2000, *Near Earth Asteroid Rendezvous (NEAR) Shoemaker* became the first space probe to orbit an asteroid (a space rock that orbits the Sun) called 433 Eros. *NEAR* (being launched left) had traveled 1.9 billion miles (3 billion km) to meet up with the asteroid, which is like traveling from the Earth to the Moon about 10 million times. The probe spent the next year orbiting around Eros, clocking up another 419 million miles (674 million km) in the process.

Almost exactly a year later, on February 12, 2001, NEAR made a very gentle landing right on top of Eros and sent dramatic photos (inset left) of the encounter back to Earth. They were the most detailed pictures of an asteroid that space scientists had yet seen.

SPACE FLIGHT TODAY

Two Shuttle astronauts pose in the payload bay while they prepare to upgrade the Hubble Space Telescope seen behind them.

More than 40 years since Yuri Gagarin first took humankind beyond Earth, space travel is much less the stuff of science fiction and much more about the practicalities of living in space. In recent years, the reusable Space Shuttle has made it much easier for people to get beyond Earth's atmosphere, and there are people working in space every day of the year inside space stations.

IS IT A ROCKET? IS IT A PLANE?

Rocket engineers have long dreamed of a spacecraft that could take off and land as easily as a plane. In 1972, President Richard Nixon (1913–94) gave the order for NASA to build a space plane. In 1977, the first Space Shuttle memorably took to the skies flying "piggy-back" on top of a jumbo jet. The Shuttle *Columbia* finally flew into space on April 12, 1981.

Standing on the launchpad, a Space Shuttle looks like an airplane strapped to a rocket. The airplane part is known as the orbiter, because it is the only part of the Shuttle that escapes Earth's atmosphere and flies into orbit. The other parts of the Shuttle are a pair of rockets that take the orbiter into space and a huge tank full of fuel and oxygen that sits in between them. The rockets are known as solid rocket boosters (SRBs). Each one is an aluminum tube packed with more than 500 tons (450 metric tons) of fuel. They burn for the first two minutes of the flight, throwing out gas at 6,000 mph (7,600 km/h). Once the SRBs are empty, the orbiter's engines continue on alone.

The Shuttle was always designed to ferry things to and from space: its official NASA name is the Space Transportation System (STS). Most of the orbiter is taken up by a payload (cargo) bay 60 feet (18.3 m) long and 15 feet (4.6 m) in diameter. Although this is large enough to hold satellites (or a couple of big trucks parked side by side), Shuttles can carry only

How things work

Launching and Landing the Shuttle

In a typical mission, the Shuttle takes off like a rocket from the Kennedy Space Center (KSC) in Florida. After spending several days in orbit roughly 190 to 330 miles (304–528 km) above Earth, it lands either at KSC or at California's Edwards Air Force Base. Although it is unpowered on its way back, the Shuttle is still traveling at around 226 mph (364 km/h) when it touches down. This is why the runway needs to be almost 3 miles (4.5 km) long. If something goes wrong the Shuttle can land at a number of long runways around the world.

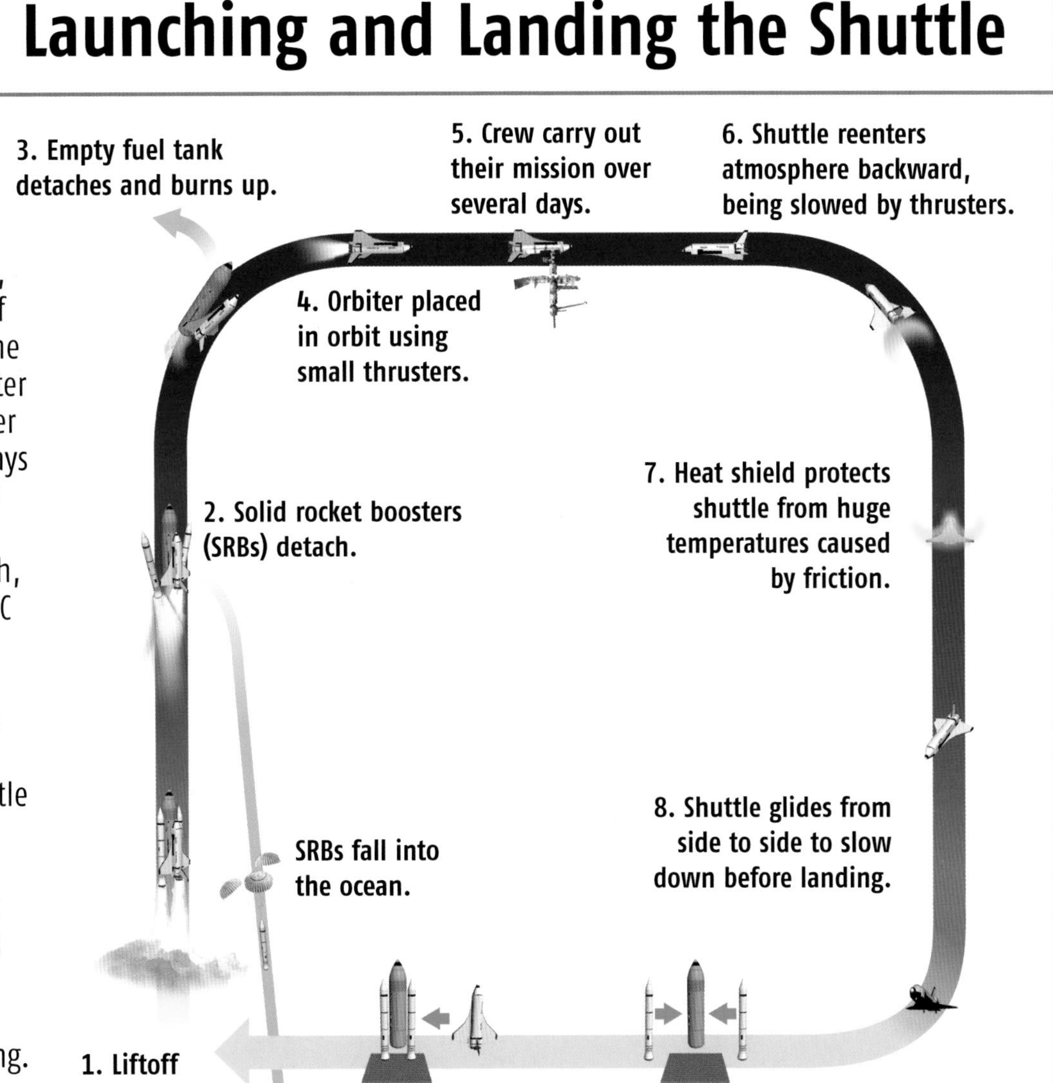

How things work

The Reusable Rocket

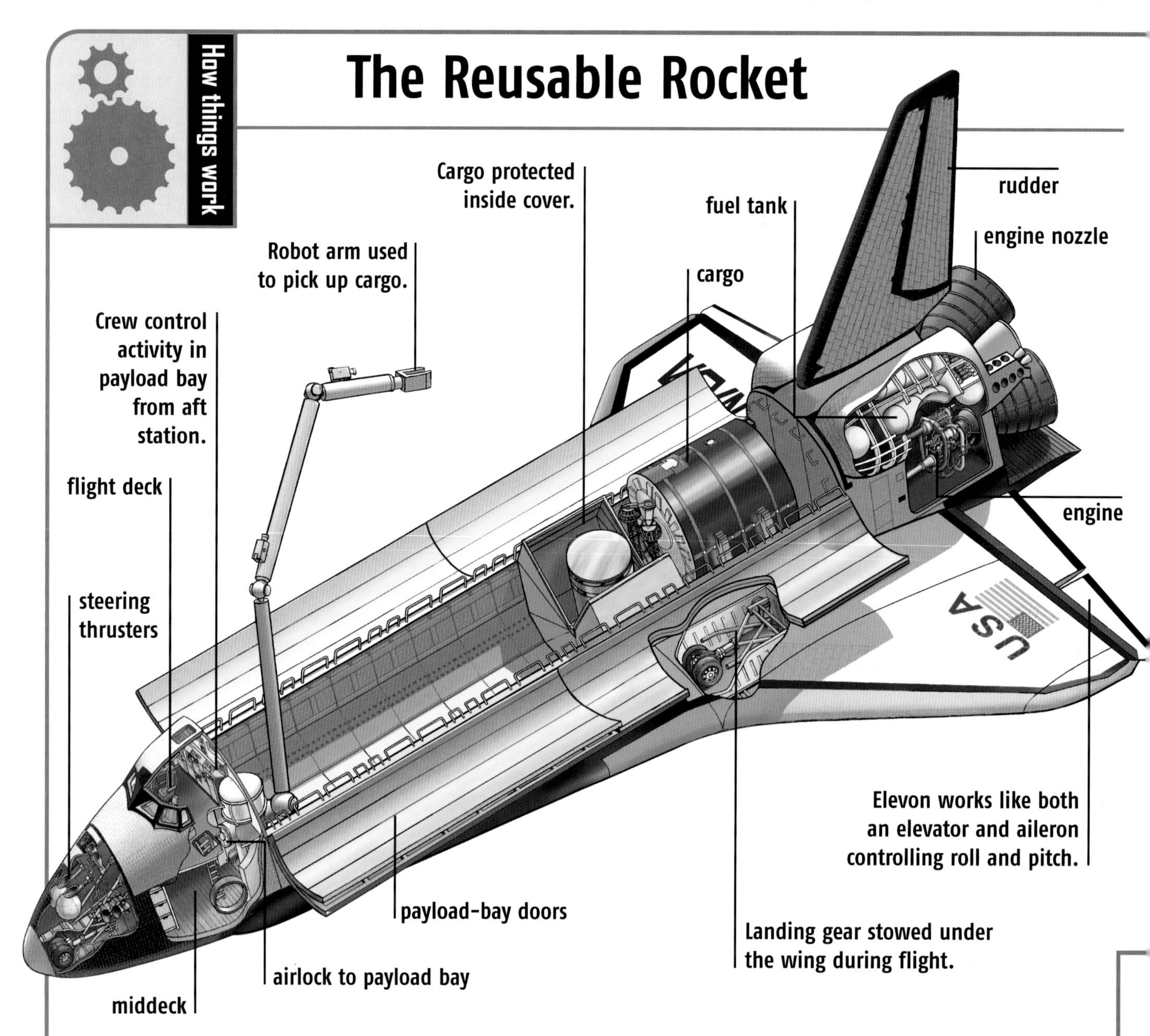

NASA has built five Shuttle orbiters at a cost of $1.5 billion each. Unlike old-style space rockets, which burned up in space like fireworks, each of these craft is designed to be reused at least 100 times. They take their names from famous sailing ships: *Columbia*, *Challenger*, *Discovery*, and *Atlantis*. *Challenger* blew up on take off in 1986 on its 25th flight and was replaced by *Endeavour* in 1991. *Columbia* broke up on reentry in 2003.

Even onboard the shuttle, space travel is a risky business. The hardest parts of each shuttle mission are launch and landing. The *Challenger* disaster was caused when flames leaked from one of the SRBs, which caused the huge fuel tank to explode. The SRB leaked because the Shuttle was launched when the weather was too cold. Getting the orbiter back to Earth in one piece is also fraught with danger. When it reenters Earth's atmosphere from space, the orbiter is traveling so fast (more than 8,250 mph; 13,200 km/h) that the air flowing past it forms a super-heated shockwave—hotter than the surface of the Sun!

Without special protection, the orbiter would burn up as it came back to Earth. So its surface is protected by thousands of heat-resistant ceramic tiles. The *Columbia* tragedy is thought to have happened because damaged tiles allowed heat to burn off the doors covering the stowed landing gear. This made the Shuttle less aerodynamic and it spun out of control and broke apart.

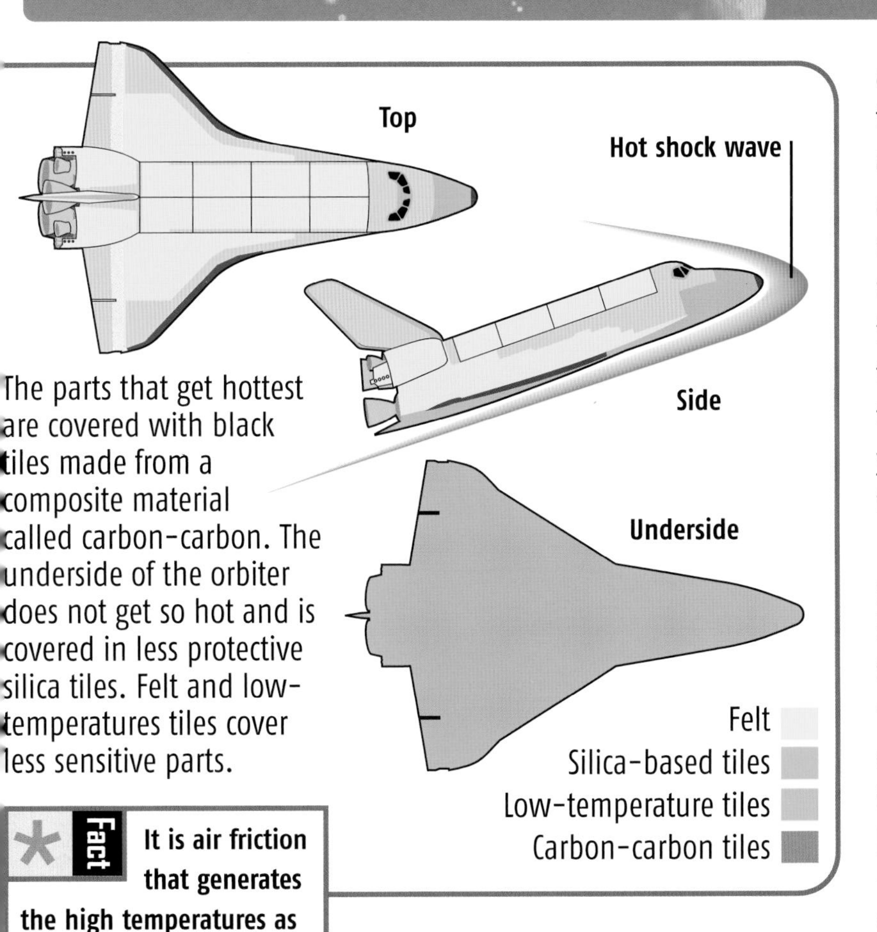

The parts that get hottest are covered with black tiles made from a composite material called carbon-carbon. The underside of the orbiter does not get so hot and is covered in less protective silica tiles. Felt and low-temperatures tiles cover less sensitive parts.

Fact **It is air friction that generates the high temperatures as the space shuttle reenters Earth's atmosphere. On the most exposed parts of the shuttle temperatures can reach an incredible 6,000°F (3,316°C).**

about a quarter as much weight into space as a large rocket, such as a Saturn V or a Russian Proton.

MISSION MILESTONES

It is more than 20 years since the Space Shuttle *Columbia* first flew into space and came back again safely. In that time, Shuttles have ventured into space more than a hundred times. The very first operational mission was from November 11 to 16, 1982, which put two commercial satellites into space. A year later, the seventh mission saw the first U.S. woman astronaut, Sally Ride (born 1951), set out on the Space Shuttle.

Some of the Shuttle's most memorable missions have involved making repairs to satellites. This usually means that one or more astronauts have to step outside the orbiter for extra-vehicular activity (EVA)—better known as a spacewalk. On the 11th Shuttle mission, in April 1984, a satellite was retrieved by the orbiter's 50-foot (15-m) robot arm, repaired in the cargo bay, and then returned to space. In November the same year, the orbiter brought two faulty satellites back to Earth.

These early successes gave NASA great confidence in the Shuttle, but the whole program was thrown into jeopardy in January 1986 when the Shuttle *Challenger* exploded about a minute after takeoff, killing seven astronauts. Flights eventually resumed in 1988. After placing the Hubble Space Telescope into orbit in 1990, the Shuttle had to return in 1993 to correct problems with the telescope's lens. There have been many other dramatic Shuttle missions. Between 1995 and 1997, the Shuttle *Atlantis* docked with Russia's *Mir* space station several times. The Shuttle's main mission today is carrying parts of the International Space Station.

The Shuttle program celebrated its 20th birthday in 2001, clocking up a total of 375 million miles (600 million km). However, in January 2003 the program was put on hold again when *Columbia*, the largest and oldest Shuttle, disintergrated on reentry, killing its seven-person crew. It is thought the heat shield became damaged during liftoff and was not able to protect the spacecraft.

SPACE STATIONS

Space Shuttle **Atlantis** *docks with the Russian* **Mir** *space station in 1995.* **Atlantis** *brought a replacement crew to the space station as part of the Shuttle-Mir program. This picture was taken from a Russian Soyuz craft that was flown around the space station and Shuttle.*

The idea of living and working in space seems routine to people today. Imagine how it must have seemed over a century ago, in 1899. This is when U.S. writer Edward Everett Hale (1822–1909) suggested the very first orbiting space station in a story called *The Brick Moon*. Without the benefit of modern materials, Hale's characters had to build their space station out of bricks and mortar. Long before the age of satellites, they jumped up and down on their artificial moon to send signals back to Earth in Morse code!

Real space stations are a lot more sophisticated. The first space station, *Salyut 1*, was launched by the Soviet Union in 1971. Its second crew stayed a record 24 days and carried out many pioneering experiments. Tragedy struck on the return to Earth, however, when the three cosmonauts were killed. Over the next decade, the Soviets sent up six more Salyut stations, which were visited by people from all over the world.

Not to be outdone, the United States built its rival *Skylab* space station out of a

Two U.S. astronauts enjoy the weightlessness on board **Skylab.** *This early space station was built inside a converted Moon rocket.*

A computer graphic showing how the completed International Space Station will look. The ISS will have a crew of seven astronauts, from 16 nations, who will spend up to six months at a time on board. When finished the space station will have as much room inside as a Boeing 747. In 2001, Russia hosted the first space tourist, Californian businessman Dennis Tito on the ISS. The price of his eight-day stay was $20 million.

modified Saturn V rocket and launched it in May 1973. During the first mission, three astronauts fixed damage to *Skylab's* solar panels that had occurred during blastoff. This momentous achievement proved that it was possible to carry out repairs to satellites in space. There were two other missions to *Skylab*, but the station fell out of its orbit in 1979 and broke apart. Shortly afterward, parts of it crashed back to Earth and narrowly missed hitting people in Australia.

When the Salyut program came to an end, the Soviet Union launched a replacement space station called *Mir* in 1986. *Mir* was more advanced and crews could live and work there for much longer periods. In 1987 and 1988 two *Mir* cosmonauts clocked up a record 366 days in space. They, like other people who stay in weightlessness for long periods, were very weak when they returned to Earth.

Mir's later years were more troubled, however. By 1997, it had suffered 1,500 problems and some major disasters, including a fire and a collision with a cargo ship that made a hole in the bulkhead. The space station was abandoned in 2000 and was destroyed in 2001 after 15 years in space.

The lessons learned on *Mir*, such as how to clean the air and deal with waste, have proved invaluable for the International Space Station (ISS), the newest and largest of space station. The first ISS module was put into space by a Russian Proton rocket in 1998. Shuttle crews have added more modules since. and the station is due to be completed in 2005.

MISSIONS OF THE FUTURE

An artist's impression of the X-33. This spacecraft never flew, but its wedge-shaped body would have behaved like a wing as it moved through the air.

Space exploration, by its very nature, is all about the future. Some of the cutting-edge technology being developed today provides a tantalizing glimpse of what may lie ahead in the space-age world of tomorrow.

AFTER THE SHUTTLE

The reusable Space Shuttle has made getting to and from space much easier than it was in the 1960s and 1970s. All the same, each shuttle mission still costs around $500 million, takes months of preparation, and carries a high degree of risk for the astronauts onboard. During the late 1990s, NASA began work with aerospace companies such as Lockheed Martin and Boeing to develop a replacement spacecraft. Several sci-fi designs for dazzling new spacecraft appeared soon afterward. Using very efficient new rocket engines, the wedge-shaped *X-33 Venture Star* would have been able to take off vertically without booster rockets before flying into space at speeds of up to Mach 15 (15 times the speed of sound; 11,000 mph or

18,000 km/h). However, after the project was plagued with technical problems and mounting costs, NASA cancelled the *X-33* and its smaller sister plane, the *X-34*, in early 2001. It has still to announce a replacement.

A concept of how the* X-43 Hyper-X *might look with its super-powerful scramjet engine. Scramjets might be used to launch spacecraft high into the atmosphere, at which point rockets would take over as it entered space.

POWER FOR TOMORROW

The key to developing faster space planes is to come up with better engines. Today's rockets seem quite old fashioned compared with some of the technologies now being developed. The biggest drawback of rockets is the need to carry their own oxygen supply as well as fuel. One new type of engine solves this problem by collecting oxygen from the air in liquid form while the craft is inside Earth's atmosphere and then using this stored oxygen supply when it gets into space. Another new engine, the "air-breathing" scramjet, lets air travel through it at supersonic speeds when it is moving through the atmosphere. This burns huge amounts of fuel, generating much more power, and creates enough thrust to propel a spacecraft to hypersonic speeds up to Mach 10. A small experimental rocket plane called the *X-43 Hyper-X* is already testing air-breathing scramjets.

The Space Future

What benefits will space bring to ordinary people? The International Space Station could lead to space hotels and space tourism. Plants may be grown in space greenhouses closer to the Sun to improve yields, while zero-gravity may provide better conditions for some types of factories. Perhaps huge solar power stations could beam their energy directly back to Earth. And space probes have already discovered valuable minerals on other planets that could prove useful to us on Earth.

We do not necessarily have to leave Earth to benefit from space. NASA can see a future where parcels are delivered anywhere in the world within two hours by a fleet of rocket planes. Tomorrow's airliners may also fly briefly into space to cut their journey times. Military planes will fly in space, too. If the wars of today are won by fighter planes that dominate the air, there is little doubt that the battles of tomorrow will be won by war machines that dominate space.

Spaceplanes of the future may have even more advanced engines than this. Solar sails are a way of using the electric or heat energy from the Sun to "sail" a spaceship through space. Ion engines also uses energy in a similar way. Other technologies include rockets that ride on laser beams or levitate (float) on magnetic tracks like hi-tech trains), and engines powered by a new generation of nuclear reactors.

WHAT WILL IT BE LIKE?
People laughed when Robert Hutchings Goddard suggested humans would one day set foot on the Moon and some of today's space-age dreams might seem just as far fetched. It is tempting to wonder what the Wright brothers would have made of a plane like the Space Shuttle if they could have shot forward in time. Would they have marveled at humanity's ingenuity and progress in the century since they took to the sky? Or would they have disappeared into their work shop to come up with something better!

How things work

Ion Engines

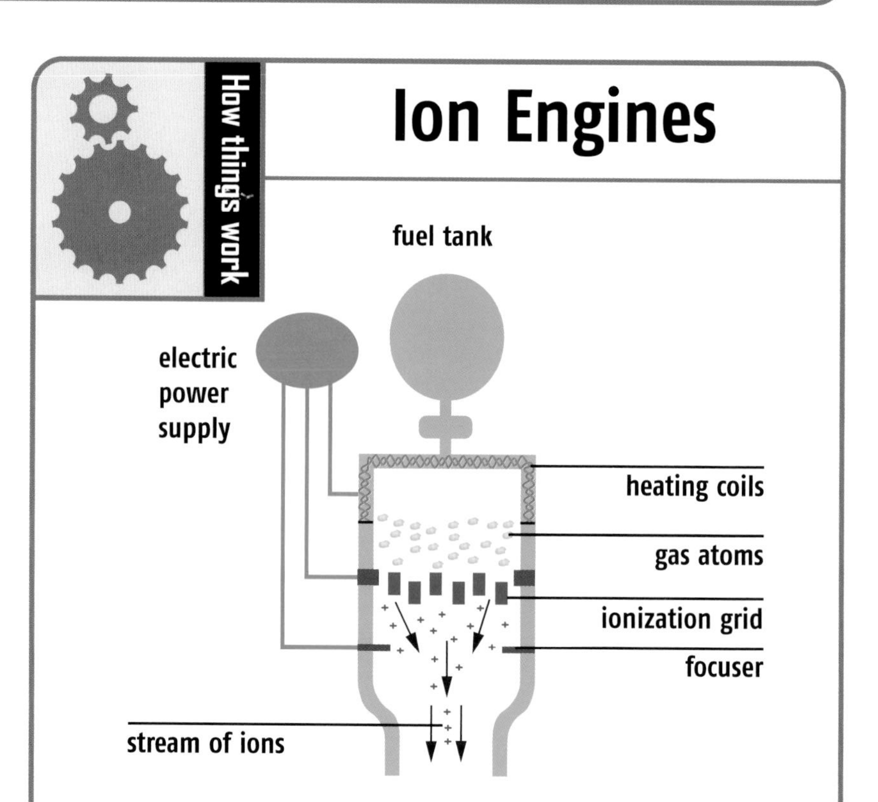

A jet engine pushes a plane forward by throwing a stream of hot exhaust gas backward. A very efficient new rocket design called an ion engine uses a similar idea, but throws out positively charged particles called ions instead of hot gas. The engine takes fuel from a tank and heats it into a gas. The gas passes over an electrically charged grid, which turns the atoms of gas into positively charged particles called ions. The ions are focused into a stream and accelerated to a very high speed by an electric field. This stream of ion produces thrust. *Deep Space 1* was the first spacecraft to be powered by an ion engine. Launched in 1998, this probe used its revolutionary engine to fly past an asteroid and a comet.

Missions to Mars

If they reach Mars, astronauts will have to stay for many weeks, perhaps in a craft like this.

People have always wanted to go to Mars—even though the dusty red planet is 50 million miles (80 million km) from Earth. The uncrewed Mariner space probes orbited Mars in the 1960s, while more sophisticated Viking probes landed on the planet's surface to analyze soil and take photographs in the 1970s.

Other Mars missions have been less successful. In 1998, NASA's $125 million *Mars Climate Orbiter* probe was destroyed when it flew too close to the red planet and burned up in its atmosphere. This very costly mistake was caused by NASA programming the craft in meters and centimeters, while the company that built it had used feet and inches! The following year, NASA lost another probe, the *Mars Polar Lander*. Although the probe reached Mars successfully, NASA lost contact with it before it landed on the surface. The probe was never heard from again.

Problems like this have made NASA very cautious about sending people to Mars. Another difficulty is the sheer cost. A 1989 study for the U.S. president estimated the cost of putting astronauts on Mars at about half a trillion dollars. Although a number of Mars missions are planned over the coming decade, all will be made by uncrewed space probes. It could be many years or even decades before people finally set foot on the red planet.

Time Line

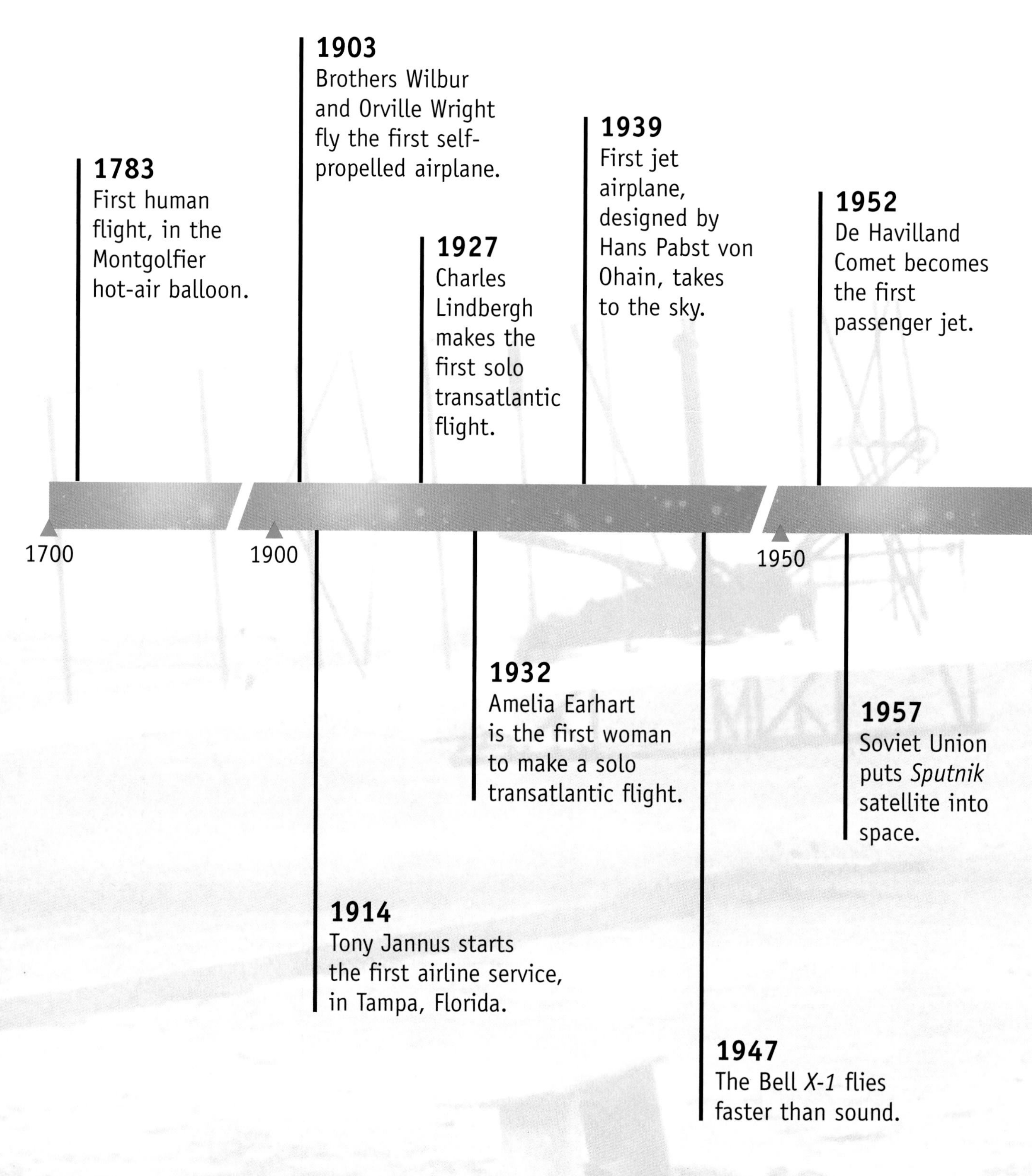

1783
First human flight, in the Montgolfier hot-air balloon.

1903
Brothers Wilbur and Orville Wright fly the first self-propelled airplane.

1914
Tony Jannus starts the first airline service, in Tampa, Florida.

1927
Charles Lindbergh makes the first solo transatlantic flight.

1932
Amelia Earhart is the first woman to make a solo transatlantic flight.

1939
First jet airplane, designed by Hans Pabst von Ohain, takes to the sky.

1947
The Bell *X-1* flies faster than sound.

1952
De Havilland Comet becomes the first passenger jet.

1957
Soviet Union puts *Sputnik* satellite into space.

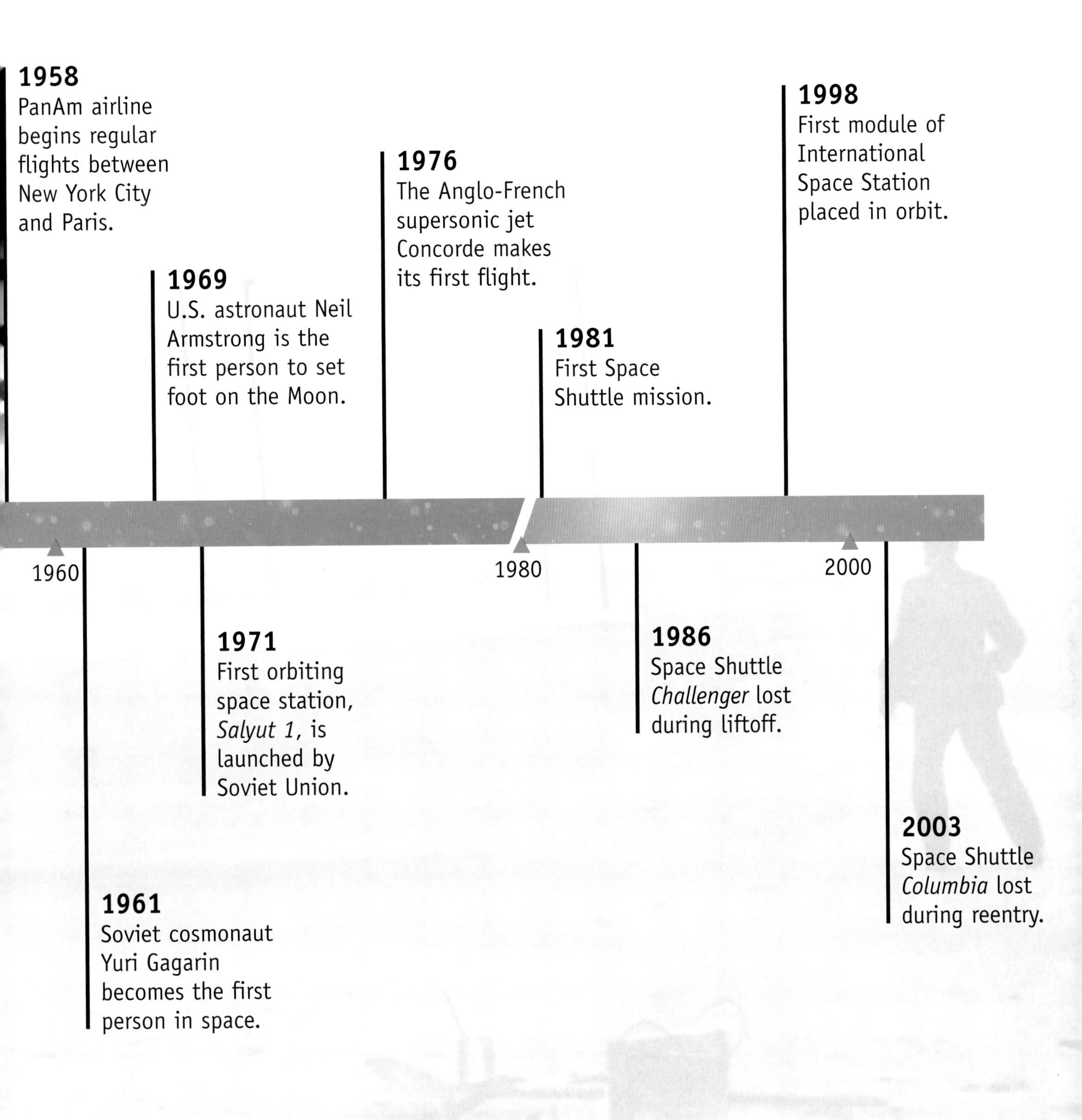

1958
PanAm airline begins regular flights between New York City and Paris.

1961
Soviet cosmonaut Yuri Gagarin becomes the first person in space.

1969
U.S. astronaut Neil Armstrong is the first person to set foot on the Moon.

1971
First orbiting space station, *Salyut 1*, is launched by Soviet Union.

1976
The Anglo-French supersonic jet Concorde makes its first flight.

1981
First Space Shuttle mission.

1986
Space Shuttle *Challenger* lost during liftoff.

1998
First module of International Space Station placed in orbit.

2003
Space Shuttle *Columbia* lost during reentry.

Glossary

aerodynamics The science of how air flows around a moving object.
airfoil The curved surface of a wing that gives an airplane its lift force.
autogyro A small airplane that also has a helicopter rotor.
biplane An airplane with two sets of wings.
Bernoulli's principle A scientific law that explains how airplane wings generate lift.
collective pitch A control lever that makes a helicopter take off or land.
combustion The process of burning fuel with oxygen in an engine.
composite A material made from two or more separated materials that combines their qualities.
cosmonaut A Soviet or Russian astronaut.
cyclic pitch The steering control on a helicopter.
dirigible A type of hot air balloon that can be steered.
drag The air resistance that slows down an aircraft.
elevator A flap on an airplane's wings that controls how quickly it takes off.
fuselage The body of an airplane.
geostationary orbit A path followed by a satellite that keeps it in the same spot above Earth all the time.
hypersonic A speed at least five times the speed of sound (Mach 5).
Mach number The number of times the speed of sound that something can fly at. Mach 1 is the same as the speed of sound, Mach 2 is twice the speed of sound, and so on.
monoplane An airplane with one set of wings.
orbit The path of a satellite.
oxidant The material that burns fuel in a rocket engine.
polar orbit The path followed by a satellite that needs to pass over every point on Earth's surface.
probe An uncrewed craft used to explore space.
rocket A reaction engine that carries its own supply of fuel and oxygen.
rotor The spinning wing that keeps a helicopter in the air.
satellite An object that moves in a path (orbit) around a planet.
scramjet A rocket engine that burns fuel at supersonic speeds.
sonic boom The noise made by an aircraft as it travels at the speed of sound.
space station A satellite that carries a human crew.
stealth A type of airplane that is especially hard to detect.
supersonic A speed greater than the speed of sound.
turbulence The disturbance that buffets an airplane around, especially at high speeds.
VSTOL Vertical/Standing Takeoff and Landing, a plane that can take off or land straight up or down or using a very short runway.

Further Resources

Books

Flight: 100 Years of Aviation by R.G. Grant and John R. Dailey. DK Publishing, 2002.

Space Shuttle: The First 20 Years by Tony Reichhardt and the Smithsonian Institution. DK Publishing, 2002.

Web Sites

Smithsonian: Aviation and Transportation
http://www.si.edu/science_and_technology/aviation_and_transportation/

NASA Human Space Flight
http://spaceflight.nasa.gov/

NASA Exploring the Universe
http://www.nasa.gov/vision/universe/features/index.html

Index

Page numbers in **bold** refer to feature spreads; those in *italics* refer to picture captions.

Picture Credits

Airbus: 44b, 46; **Corbis**: 35, 59, Archivo Iconografico, S.A. 6, David Baranet 30, Bettmann 14, 34, 37, 51, 67b, 68, Leonard De Selva 10, Patrik Giardino 47, Dave G. Houser 11, Philippa Lewis; Edifice 7, Joe McBride 27, Museum of Flight 32, Geray Sweeney 62; **Corbis Sygma**: Alain Nogues 50; **Defense Digest**: 61t; **Getty Images**: 63, Frank Whitney 8; **NASA**: 2, 65, 67t, 70, 71, 72t, 72b, 78, 85t, 85b, 89, Dryden Flight Research Center 43, 56, 86, 87, Human Space Flight Center 80, Jet Propulsion Library 76, Johnson Space Center 66, 74, 84, NEAR Project (JHU/APC) 79b; **NOAA**: Commander John Bortniak 12b; **Robert Hunt Library**: 12t, 16, 20, 21, 22, 24, 26, 28, 29t, 29b, 42, 44t, 49b; **Rolls Royce plc**: 38, 48, 58; **Science & Society**: Science Museum 23, 41; **Skyscan**: B. Pitman 18; **Sylvia Cordaiy Photo Library**: Howard Rolstone 33, Chris Parker 40; **TRH Pictures**: 17, Martin Baker 57, Bell 53, Lockheed-Martin 60, 61b, Dave Willis 49t.